The Teacher's Guide to Resolving School Bullying

of related interest

Emily Is Being Bullied, What Can She Do?
A Story and Anti-Bullying Guide for Children and Adults to Read Together
Helen Cowie, Harriet Tenenbaum and Ffion Jones
Illustrated by Ffion Jones
ISBN 978 1 78592 548 1
eISBN 978 1 78450 948 4

How to Do Restorative Peer Mediation in Your School
A Quick Start Kit
Bill Hansberry and Christie-Lee Hansberry
Foreword by Marg Thorsborne
ISBN 978 1 78592 384 5
eISBN 978 1 78450 736 7

Be Bully Free
A Hands-On Guide to How You Can Take Control
Michael Panckridge and Catherine Thornton
ISBN 978 1 78592 282 4
eISBN 978 1 78450 583 7

A Practical Introduction to Restorative Practice in Schools
Theory, Skills and Guidance
Bill Hansberry
Foreword by Margaret Thorsborne
ISBN 978 1 84905 707 3
eISBN 978 1 78450 232 4

The Teacher's Guide to
Resolving School Bullying

Evidence-Based Strategies and Pupil-Led Interventions

Elizabeth Nassem

Jessica Kingsley *Publishers*
London and Philadelphia

First published in 2020
by Jessica Kingsley Publishers
73 Collier Street
London N1 9BE, UK
and
400 Market Street, Suite 400
Philadelphia, PA 19106, USA

www.jkp.com

Library of Congress Cataloging in Publication Data
A CIP catalog record for this book is available from the Library of Congress

British Library Cataloguing in Publication Data
A CIP catalogue record for this book is available from the British Library

ISBN 978 1 78592 419 4
eISBN 978 1 78450 785 5

Printed and bound in Great Britain

This book is dedicated to the individuals who have felt hurt by bullying and want to do more to resolve it. I hope that my book will help you.

Contents

Acknowledgements

I thank the schools that allowed me to implement my research and the participants from whom I learnt so much. I am grateful to the children who feature in this book for your honesty and sincerity. You have taught me so much about bullying and have a wealth of resources to help us understand and address it.

Thank you to my mum, who has been my greatest source of support and encouragement. I thank you for your love and guidance and helping me to have the faith, courage and strength to strive for this. I also thank my dad for your support and advice. You have had such belief in me that has helped me to stay focused and have confidence.

Chapter 1

Introduction

Aims and Scope

The Teacher's Guide to Resolving School Bullying will help you address the mundane, challenging and complex issues of bullying with which you are frequently confronted but which are often neglected by researchers and practitioners. Such complex cases of bullying include teasing which *may* cause distress, persistent conflict between 'friends', and hostility between teachers and pupils. These experiences are often considered as too nuanced for traditional researchers to examine. Traditional research on school bullying usually focuses on statistics which suppress the child's voice and overlook their unique experiences. Furthermore, they cannot tell us enough about how to deal with the underlying reasons behind the bullying. However, this book will help you understand children's lived experiences and resolve bullying by dealing with the fundamental issues which contribute to it.

Many people know what it feels like to be bullied. Despite a wealth of research and interventions to combat bullying, it is still a common problem in schools (The Children's Society 2016) and is associated with depression, anxiety and even suicide. Although schools are legally obliged to tackle bullying (Department for Education 2017), school practitioners may not have had adequate guidance or training on how to do so. Consequently, attempts to tackle bullying often focus on the more obvious forms of physical aggression rather than considering more nuanced experiences which are much more prevalent in school. There has recently been an increase in theoretical approaches to understanding school bullying which consider the complexities involved (for example, Walton 2010; Schott and Sondergaard 2014; Kousholt and Fisker 2015). However, they do not usually include the child's input in sufficient depth.

I have researched bullying for more than ten years and implemented interventions in schools since 2014. My most recent interventions have found that the most effective approaches reposition children as active agents and enable children to be instrumental in understanding and resolving their bullying. We can do much more to involve children in creating an anti-bullying culture – this book will help you get started.

Rather than focusing on the negative characteristics of a pathologized minority identified as 'victims' and 'bullies', as traditional research tends to do, this book considers how all children are affected by bullying because of the fear, tensions and disruption to learning it can cause (Lurie and Zylke 2001), for example, if they are frightened of being humiliated for answering a question wrongly in class. In *The Teacher's Guide to Resolving School Bullying*, new approaches are recommended which have arisen from my research into the complexity of school bullying from the child's perspective. These approaches will help school practitioners who are responsible for dealing with bullying to feel confident and equipped to do so, as recommended by Ofsted (2012).

What Is Bullying?

Bullying is usually defined as a specific form of aggression which is repeated, intentional and where the bully clearly has power (physical or psychological) over the victim. This definition was developed by Olweus (1993) and is considered to be the traditional approach because the majority of researchers in school bullying use this definition (for example, Terasahjo and Salmivalli 2003; Rowe *et al.* 2008; Gumpel *et al.* 2014).

Olweus' (1993) definition, however, is problematic. Lee (2006) challenges the concept of repetition by arguing that just one experience of maltreatment can have side-effects such as fear and distress long after the maltreatment has been experienced. The intentionality dimension is over-simplified as it can be difficult to determine if children consciously aim to harm others. Many say they 'didn't mean it' (Ofsted 2003). Furthermore, how much does it matter whether or not bullying is intentional? Children can be just as hurt by inadvertent remarks as deliberate attempts to cause harm (Cullingford and Brown 1995). There are cases when it is difficult to establish a clear imbalance of power, for example, when there is maltreatment between pupils in the same class who appear to have the same physical, psychological and intellectual strength. Furthermore, children who are perceived as having less physical or psychological strength than their peers can still abuse their power over them. Power can be fluid in relationships, providing a multitude of opportunities for power to be wielded. In *The Teacher's Guide to Resolving School Bullying,* bullying is constructed as a slippery concept which is multi-layered, nuanced and interpreted differently by individuals rather than as specific aggression identified by the traditional approach.

Children experience bullying in more complex and subtle ways than traditional approaches allow. Consider the following issues: when children are calling each other names are they 'having a laugh' or does something more serious lie beneath it? Two friends are arguing and they both say they are being bullied by each other. You have noticed they seem to be arguing a lot, almost on a daily basis. However, when you see them the next day they are playing together. Who is bullying whom, or is this nothing to worry about? A group of boys are playing a game where they whip others with sticks – is this bullying, violence or just a game (Nassem 2015)? Evidently, in certain cases, it is difficult to clearly establish whether children are being bullied. Morita (1996) points out that teasing may add 'lightness to the day' and be considered as humorous, but there are also cases where children have committed suicide because of it.

Instead of objectively aiming to distinguish bullying from other forms of aggression, then, why don't we examine how children perceive the maltreatment they endure? Arguably, teasing becomes bullying when individuals become distressed by it. It is important, therefore, for children to develop empathy, so that they understand the effect their behaviour has on others – and when that behaviour is causing distress. However, teasing which appears playful could still be bullying. Some children who feel distressed by teasing may conceal their hurt feelings such as laughing when they are taunted and saying that they do not feel bullied. To help you deal with these complexities, the 'empathetic understanding' approach explained in this book will help you investigate beyond the surface of what children are saying about the maltreatment they might be experiencing. This will help you learn more about the extent to which children are being bullied so you can address it more effectively.

Although there are likely to be some commonalities in how individuals experience bullying, each case of bullying is unique, and often involves a multitude of ambiguities and nuances. To understand the diverse ways that individuals experience school bullying, consider what behaviours children are experiencing which might be bullying, such as being called unpleasant names, being teased and/or experiencing physical violence. These behaviours are considered to be characteristics of school bullying which are on a spectrum that ranges from mild to severe bullying and includes 'grey' areas.

Please see Appendix 1 for a list of characteristics of school bullying which includes examples of behaviours and experiences associated with bullying. This list is not exhaustive but will provide a framework to help clarify your understanding. These characteristics developed from reviewing the literature on bullying and speaking with children about what bullying consists of. You can extend your knowledge of what the characteristics of bullying are by asking which behaviours they consider to be bullying. Both covert (for example, subtly participating in ostracizing others) and overt maltreatment (for example physical violence which clearly caused distress to others) are seen as bullying. Aggression which is repeated, intentional and involves a clear imbalance in power is considered as clearly bullying. By developing a list of the criteria and characteristics associated with bullying you will develop a more flexible and nuanced understanding. Appendix 2 provides a definition of school bullying developed from the research in this book, and Appendix 3 provides a diagram showing the multi-faceted model of school bullying to represent how bullying is constructed in this book.

Bullying between Pupils and School Practitioners

Unlike most other books on bullying, *The Teacher's Guide to Resolving School Bullying* examines the nuanced positioning of school practitioners in tackling bullying. School practitioners can feel pressured to ensure all students achieve the educational standards expected of them which can contribute to tensions with pupils who are not achieving those standards. Subsequently, these children can feel 'picked on' by teachers which can contribute to them being hostile and, in some cases, aggressive towards their teachers. I found this was particularly pertinent in children from working-class backgrounds who had learning difficulties. These children were usually from particularly economically deprived working-class backgrounds and their parents were usually unemployed or earned low salaries. They often preferred to conform to their peer group and be connected to their local community rather than obey their teachers and achieve academic success. Most of these children were males but there were some females from this socio-economic background who also felt frequently 'picked on' by their teachers. This book, unlike most others on school bullying, also examines how teachers can be bullied by pupils. Techniques to support you if you feel victimized or are perceived as 'picking on' pupils are outlined. The strategy 'empowering practitioners' is provided to strengthen your resources and support network to deal with bullying authoritatively. The 'healthy relationships' approach also aims to encourage pupils, and pupils and staff, to interact with each other more respectfully.

Systemic Bullying

Although most other books only focus on maltreatment which involves a clear imbalance of power between individuals (Olweus 1993), this book examines how power inherent in bullying is more fluid and nuanced by drawing on the work of Foucault (1979, 1980). For Foucault, power exists in all relationships and involves power struggles. Although no one holds complete power, there are hierarchies and inequalities in school and society such as in social class where certain individuals and groups are dominated.

The multi-faceted model presented in this book primarily examines bullying between pupils, pupils and teachers, and systemic bullying. The concept of systemic bullying situates bullying within an institutional and societal context rather than just focusing on individuals. Systemic bullying comprises institutional structures of school (such as punitive disciplinary methods) and societal inequalities (such as in social class and gender) which can target certain children, marginalize them, cause them distress and be perceived as bullying (Nassem 2012, 2017). An example of systemic bullying is when children in the lowest class are distressed because they feel 'thick'. Although systemic bullying operates beyond the individual level of pupils and staff, it is entangled with these interactions, for example, when pupils upset those who are in the lowest streams because they call them 'thick' or if a child with dyslexia who is embarrassed about their reading difficulties is excluded by their teacher for not reading out loud in class. Strategies to deal with the multi-faceted nature of bullying are included in this book.

Power is examined through concepts of normalization and surveillance (Foucault 1979, 1980). According to Foucault, normalization and surveillance are significant forms of disciplinary power which have replaced the sovereign central power of the king. Disciplinary power operates covertly through systems of social control by rules, procedures and regulation (Foucault 1979). Disciplinary power influences how individuals behave, and perceive themselves and others. It is institutionalized through coercion and acceptance.

Normalization creates divisions between normality and difference through establishing hierarchies which rank individuals, for example, through assessment results. Pupils who are constructed as 'different' can be perceived as aberrant as they develop awareness of what standards are expected. This can marginalize those who do not achieve the standards expected of them and create an abnormal, shameful class (Foucault 1979). If this process causes children distress it can be construed as systemic bullying.

Although all individuals are observed by others, those who do not conform to social and educational norms experience surveillance which increases their visibility and experience of being judged. Through surveillance and normalization, individuals can become targeted by pupils and school staff, marginalized and subject to increasing punishment and pressure to conform when they are perceived as not achieving the social and/or educational norms expected of them (Foucault 1979). This book examines how traditional ways of identifying 'bullies' can be used to target and punish working-class males with learning difficulties who are already marginalized.

Often anti-bullying practices in schools focus on punishing pupils who are overtly aggressive such as excluding those identified as 'bullies' before investigating what contributed to the aggressive response in the first place. Such a crude and punitive approach perpetuates bullying (Nassem 2012, 2017). Recommendations are provided of how you can encourage children to resist power which is exercised over them and exercise their agency in terms of how they respond to bullying. A 'take responsibility' approach is described in this book to support children to make informed decisions about their behaviour and realize the impact it has on others.

Interventions are recommended to help you to protect children who are vulnerable to bullying and improve how it is dealt with in school, through approaches such as the 'Mentoring for "Bullies"' programme. Resources to help you overcome systemic bullying, and deal with the underlying issues which contribute to bullying, have not previously been covered in a comprehensive text on children's experiences of bullying but are provided here.

Evidence Base

The original knowledge base underpinning this book is from qualitative research and evidence-based interventions with pupils which have been successfully implemented by the author. Pseudonyms are used for all names of pupils, school practitioners and schools in order to maintain anonymity. The substantial emphasis on the child's voice contrasts to the traditional approach which tends to reduce children's experiences to statistics. Data is drawn from observations, focus groups, and individual interviews with children aged 9 to 16 from different education establishments such as primary and secondary state schools, a private school and a Pupil Referral Unit (PRU). The first part of this book presents data drawn from my research into children's perceptions and experiences of bullying. The second part of this book (Chapters 6 to 8) focuses specifically on data from my most recent pupil-led evidence-based interventions. Some children in this book were interviewed more than once to develop greater insight into their responses. In Carfield Primary Academy children were interviewed four times to develop and evaluate a pupil-led intervention based on their experiences of bullying. Resources to help you implement these interventions and support the professional development of your colleagues are provided.

Traditional and New Approaches to Combat Bullying

To my knowledge, interventions to combat bullying have had only modest success which indicates there is much to learn about making interventions more successful (Smith 2011; Department for Education 2017). Established interventions used to tackle bullying include: the shared concern approach by Pikas (1989), restorative justice and KiVa[1] which was developed by Christina Salmivalli.

The shared concern approach (Pikas 1989) involves a teacher having conversations with the victim, the bully and other pupils involved in the bullying. The teacher follows a structured script with each pupil, leading to a mutual agreement that the bullied pupil is unhappy with the situation and concluding by each pupil agreeing to help improve the situation. However, schools that have used this method have found that some older primary age pupils cannot suggest ways to improve the situation. They need adults to take a more directive role (Thompson, Arora and Sharp 2002). The pupil-led approaches in this book will help you provide sufficient support to pupils.

---

1   KiVa is an acronym for 'Kiusaamista Vastaan' which means 'against bullying' in Finnish and the word 'kiva' is also a Finnish word for 'nice'.

Restorative justice aims to repair the harm caused by a particular offence or incident. Through structured communication, victims and perpetrators can discuss with each other how they were affected by the incident and explore what they will do to repair the harm caused (Youth Justice Board 2004). However, Littlechild (2003) found that it was difficult for those individuals involved to seek agreement on how to move forwards and resolve the issues concerned with bullying.

KiVa is a particularly rigid approach which has universal actions that are applied in all cases, at both class and school level, and structured actions that are used to address confirmed cases of bullying. Training, resources, class lessons, online activities, and parental advice and support are provided. In specific cases of bullying a member of the KiVa team first meets the victim to gain understanding of the situation and offer support. The team then meets individually with the 'bully'/'bullies'. In this meeting the 'bully' is asked to commit to actions to help the victim (Hutchings and Clarkson 2017). However, this approach is asking for a significant change in their behaviour from being abusive to suddenly becoming supportive. Furthermore, 'grey' areas and complex cases of bullying which you are probably confronted with on a daily basis, such as when bullying involves a large group and there is not a clearly identified perpetrator, are, in my opinion, not adequately addressed through KiVa.

The Teacher's Guide to Resolving School Bullying contains original and evidence-based strategies which you can easily adapt to understanding and dealing with bullying in your school. This contrasts to the more commonly used interventions such as the method of shared concern, restorative justice and KiVa which can be quite generalized and restricted. Consequently, they may not be sufficiently adaptable to deal with the specific issues of bullying in your school. Furthermore, they tend to focus on bullying which has already escalated. This book will help you deal with a broad spectrum of cases, including those which are mild and ambiguous, which traditional interventions tend to overlook.

The original strategies used to tackle bullying in this book will now be outlined. These approaches will help you understand the underlying issues which contribute to bullying whilst also paying particular attention to the child's voice. Such approaches will help you manage the institutional, social and interpersonal issues which contribute to bullying rather than just focusing on specific reported cases of bullying (whereas most interventions primarily focus on the latter).

Summary of Strategies
'Mentoring for "Bullies"'

This is an in-depth programme of support for pupils who persistently engage in bullying to reflect upon their behaviour and learn how to behave more respectfully. Mentoring focuses on understanding the underlying reasons why children engage in bullying. It supports individuals to exercise their agency and make informed decisions about their behaviour.

'Take responsibility'

This is a method which encourages children to realize the impact their behaviour has on their peers and school practitioners. Through staff supporting pupils to become more mindful of how their behaviour can inadvertently hurt others it can help prevent an over-reliance on overt punishment. 'Take responsibility' aims to encourage pupils and practitioners to work both individually and collaboratively to reduce bullying. It has been successfully used to help those who persistently engaged in bullying to transform their behaviour.

'Pupil-led approaches'

This strategy consists of pupils having a leading role in enhancing understanding of their lived experiences of bullying and developing strategies to tackle it. Pupils contribute to the design, implementation and evaluation of anti-bullying initiatives. They are supported to become positive role-models who challenge bullying, interact more respectfully with pupils and staff, and help those who are victimized.

'Empathetic understanding'

The 'empathetic understanding' strategy is for pupils, and pupils and staff, to enhance their knowledge of one another's perspective and learn about the underlying reasons which are contributing to their behaviour. It involves pupils, and pupils and staff, having open and reflective dialogue with one another. Conversations focus on why individuals are behaving in ways that can be perceived as hurtful and how this is making individuals feel. This approach can help those involved in bullying to fully understand each other's perspective when they listen to and respond to the views of others. The open and reflective dialogue can be used to enhance the voice of pupils. It can also support practitioners to more thoroughly investigate children's experiences of bullying which are usually overlooked and provide bespoke interventions to deal with their specific issues with bullying. Through engaging in reflective dialogue with pupils and colleagues, the 'empathetic understanding' approach can be used to support school practitioners in protecting vulnerable groups from bullying, such as working-class males with learning difficulties.

'Healthy relationships'

The 'healthy relationships' strategy focuses on improving the social interactions between pupils, and pupils and school practitioners. Interventions are recommended for schools to embed learning about respectful relationships into the curriculum, support pupils to have a positive outlet if they have negative feelings and resolve conflict between pupils, and pupils and staff, peacefully. It can encourage pupils to develop respectful social interactions and challenge normalized practices in school which enable bullying. 'Healthy relationships' can be used to help resolve conflicts in the earliest stages before they escalate into severe bullying.

'Empowering practitioners'

'Empowering practitioners' aims to enhance understanding of the complex positioning of school practitioners and strengthen their resources to deal with bullying authoritatively. Recommendations are provided to help school practitioners to enhance their knowledge, skills and support network to deal with bullying effectively.

Outline of Following Chapters

Chapter 2 focuses on helping you understand pupils' perceptions of bullying and resolve their complex experiences of it. You will learn about the underlying reasons why children engage in bullying and develop effective strategies to deal with it. 'Empathetic understanding' is introduced to help you learn more about children's experiences of bullying in your school and investigate it. My original doctoral research finding is analyzed; this discovered that none of the children in my study identified themselves as 'bullies' (Nassem 2012, 2017). To help pupils to realize the effect their maltreatment has on others, new interventions such as 'take responsibility' are presented. My research finding that pupils felt bullying was commonplace and enmeshed within their everyday experience of school is discussed. The 'healthy relationships' strategy is outlined to encourage pupils to develop respectful social interactions with each other and challenge normalized practices which enable bullying.

The third chapter examines how to empower school practitioners to effectively resolve bullying. The complex positioning of how school practitioners are situated to respond to bullying is considered. The 'empowering practitioners' approach is explained which will help you enhance your knowledge and support network to deal authoritatively with bullying. The 'healthy relationships' method is outlined to include ways pupils and practitioners can perceive each other more positively and interact more respectfully. The 'empathetic understanding' approach is expanded here to encourage pupils and practitioners to enhance their understanding of one another's position and perspective. Advice on how bullying between pupils and practitioners can be addressed in anti-bullying policies are also provided.

Chapter 4 will help you understand systemic bullying and collaborate with colleagues and pupils to combat it. This chapter will discuss the institutional and societal factors inherent in school which contribute to bullying and explain how these problems can be overcome. How the institutional context of school can perpetuate bullying is examined; for example, overt forms of punishment can contribute to bullying escalating, and the restricted voice of pupils is strongly associated with bullying. Societal inequalities inherent in school which are associated with bullying such as social class and gender are also analyzed. This chapter will help you resolve some of the issues of bullying which are associated with social class, intellectual ability and gender. Strategies for schools to challenge inequalities pupils may experience are outlined. This includes how the voice of pupils can be enhanced to resolve bullying and reduce overt forms of punishment through establishing a 'system of dialogue'. How 'Mentoring for "Bullies"' can support individuals who are involved in a vicious cycle of bullying to learn how to behave more respectfully is discussed.

Chapter 5 provides resources for the professional development of school practitioners to deal with children's complex cases of bullying, based on my research, and anti-bullying strategies. This chapter will be useful for practitioners who wish to share good practice with colleagues and/or provide professional development in how to understand and deal with complex issues of bullying between pupils, teachers and pupils, and systemic bullying. Examples of materials to use in training presentations, case studies and scenarios are included.

Chapter 6 presents a case study of one of my first in-depth projects where I worked with pupils in a secondary school to resolve bullying in their school. The first 'Mentoring for "Bullies"' programme which is used for those who persistently engage in bullying to transform their behaviour is discussed. A pupil-led anti-bullying campaign was developed for children who had engaged in bullying but wanted to transform their behaviour and become positive role-models. Recommendations for schools to draw upon different expertise to reduce overt forms of punishment are provided. Details of the benefits and obstacles that were encountered will be explained. Further recommendations to develop this project are specified towards the end of this chapter.

In Chapter 7 the implementation of a pupil-led approach in a primary school is discussed; here children had a central role in designing and delivering interventions to tackle their experiences of school bullying. This intervention has also been informed through consultations with school practitioners. In Chapter 8 this pupil-led intervention is evaluated by pupils and school practitioners, and advice is provided about how you can adapt this intervention to the specific issues of bullying in your school.

The conclusion in Chapter 9 draws together the key themes and strategies for dealing with bullying that emerged from the book as a whole. Finally, the appendices include additional resources that have been devised and implemented to help you deal more effectively with bullying, such as a presentation to train colleagues; questions to ask children about their experiences of bullying; and examples of sessions you can provide to implement the mentoring and pupil-led anti-bullying programme. Appendices 7–14, which list questions to use with children and staff, are available to download at www.jkp.com/catalogue/book/9781785924194.

Chapter 2

Pupils' Complex Perceptions and Experiences of Bullying

Introduction

This chapter will help you understand pupils' perceptions and experiences of bullying, learn why children engage in bullying, and the complexity of their involvement in bullying. Guidance is provided to help you learn more about children's experiences of bullying in your school and enhance their understanding of the perspectives of those victimized. Strategies are outlined to help you encourage pupils to take more responsibility for their behaviour and the effect it has on others, and develop healthier relationships with other pupils through more respectful interactions.

Perceptions and Experiences of School Bullying: The Evidence

Name-calling and teasing: the nuances

When you decide whether certain behaviours are bullying, consider each case individually and how the individuals involved feel about these behaviours. Name-calling (i.e. referring to individuals through labels which are usually of a negative nature) is a characteristic associated with bullying. One of the pupils I interviewed, Nicole, directly referred to the name-calling she experienced as bullying: 'There's boys bullying me… [they] call me names all the time…[like] big nose' (Year 10, Parklane School). However, Paul did not consider name-calling as bullying: 'a bit of name-calling but…not really bullying' (Year 7, Highcross Private School). Nicole indicated that her bullying was persistent, with an imbalance of power between her and the boys. However, Paul highlights how Nicole's experience may appear to an outsider if they witnessed her being called names occasionally. Although Nicole experienced name-calling which insulted her personal appearance and caused her distress Paul did not report being called hurtful names. I have found children who are persistently called hurtful names are more likely to automatically refer to name-calling as bullying than those who are occasionally called names. Name-calling is bullying when it causes distress to those targeted. However, children who feel distressed by being teased or called names may not necessarily tell you or show you how they feel. In fact, they may conceal their hurt feelings. Melanie explains how she 'has a laugh' with Lee and, at the beginning of the interview, clearly states that there isn't any bullying in school:

> Interviewer: Do you think there's bullying in this school?
>
> Melanie: No, nothing at all. I think everyone has a laugh with each other, it's like with me and Lee Baker he'll take piss out of me, I'll take piss out of him but we always end up laughing about it... Only thing pisses me off is Lee Baker, all he does at school is 'my mum's bought me this, my mum's bought me other'. He'll always say it to me, and I just sit there upset and keep it inside. 'Well, what does your mum buy you; fuck all?', and he'll know he'll be winding me up but I won't bite on that, if I do I'll honestly just kick and punch him...so, I turn around, 'well, you're a spoilt little bastard, aren't you?' He goes 'I'd prefer to be spoilt than not spoilt' and I'll just fuck it me and I'll just start laughing.
>
> (Melanie, Year 11, Priory Lane PRU)

From an observer's perspective, the interaction between Melanie and Lee might appear confusing. The mutual laughter indicates a sign of friendship and there does not seem to be a clear power imbalance. However, the teasing and tormenting observed indicates that bullying may be present. Through providing Melanie with space and time to expand her dialogue she explained how she felt distressed when Lee teased her. Lee's comments made her feel angry and although she challenged him, she repressed her anger and concealed it through laughter. The only way I became aware of Melanie's distress was by giving her time to talk in more detail about her interactions with Lee.

Teasing is often ambiguous and is not always clearly bullying, particularly when children don't appear to be upset; in these cases teasing is a 'grey' area. However, teasing which upsets individuals is considered to be bullying. Peter felt profoundly distressed, ashamed and self-conscious because of the derogatory and homophobic names he was called to the extent that he attempted suicide as a consequence:

I get bullied because of my voice and my weight, [they] call me 'gay' and 'fat'... I don't like being different to everybody. I won't walk around without a coat because I don't want everybody looking at me; I took an overdose once because it all got on top of me.

(Peter, Year 10, Parklane School)

Peter was persistently bullied and his experience of bullying followed the pattern of bullying of lesbian, gay and bisexual individuals because it is perpetuated more by groups rather than individuals (Rivers and Cowie 2006). However, deciding whether several people watching Peter is bullying is an ambiguous area. Peter's experience of bullying has put his life at risk and has seeped into how he perceives himself as repulsive and unworthy (Nassem 2017).

Although the traditional approach to bullying uses the concept of intentionality to 'exclude non-serious negative actions' (Olweus 1993, p.9), individuals can be hurt when people are not being serious. In some cases, children are not always certain whether acts of teasing are intentional; many claim they didn't mean it (Ofsted 2003). 'There's people that just think that it's OK to bully people and then at the end stop and say, "oh, it was only a joke"' (Jessica, Year 7, Highcross Private School). Olweus (1993) does not explain how to investigate whether children intend to cause harm. Furthermore, how much does it matter whether individuals mean to cause harm? What matters is how people feel as a consequence of the behaviour. I have found, from my research, that most children do not engage in bullying simply to cause harm. Rather they are usually motivated to achieve other goals such as being popular within their circle; this is discussed further in the 'Why Do Children Bully?' section later in this chapter.

We need a more nuanced understanding of the concept of intentionality; individuals do not always know the difference between intentional and unintentional maltreatment, and it can be very difficult to prove. To overcome this problem, encourage children to reflect on how their behaviour can inadvertently cause significant harm to individuals so they are more aware of the impact their behaviour has on others. This process can help them make more informed decisions about how they choose to behave.

When children realize they are causing significant distress to others and they did not intentionally intend to cause harm one would expect that they would stop engaging in behaviour which is causing upset. To help children realize the impact of their behaviour, those who feel hurt can explain to those who hurt them how they feel as a consequence of their behaviour. There may also be signs of distress in children who are targeted. Children who are aware that they are causing unnecessary distress and continue to do so when they can easily change their behaviour are likely to be engaging in bullying which is intentional. However, if victimized children conceal their distress then they may not know they are causing harm. This highlights the importance of supporting those who are in conflict with one another to have respectful conversations about how they feel about their interactions and agree how they will communicate with each other more respectfully in future. Anti-bullying policies might be improved by stating that bullying can be intentional or unconscious, or by including a more detailed and nuanced description of the concept of intentionality which has been discussed.

Physical violence and bullying

The traditional approach considers physical violence as bullying only when it is intentional, repeated and involves a clear imbalance of power. In this book, physically violent interactions are characteristics on a continuum of bullying. This continuum of bullying ranges from mild to severe bullying and includes 'grey' areas. Physically violent interactions involve an abuse of physical power which can cause physical and/or psychological harm. Aggression towards an object which does not cause distress to individuals is not considered as bullying. The extent to which physical violence is bullying depends on individual experiences and the level of harm imposed or experienced.

Some children, such as Alex, similarly to Myers (2006), directly associated the violence they experienced from other children as bullying. Alex considers being 'hit in the head' by a 'couple of lads' with 'planks of wood' who were also chucking bricks at him as bullying: 'When they're with their mates they start bullying you.' Alex was left with bruises on his face as a consequence: 'I got a mushed up [i.e. bruised] face.' There is a clear imbalance in power here because several boys are victimizing one boy and using objects to cause more severe harm. Although the violence does not seem to be repeated, Alex fears that 'they'll do it again'. I argue that maltreatment does not have to be repeated if the victim continues to feel frightened (Monks *et al.* 2009*)*. Fear of further maltreatment is a side-effect of bullying. For some children, being frightened of being beaten was part of their everyday experience. In the PRU, Caleb (Year 10) reported that 'every corner you go around you have to be suspicious in case someone tries hitting you'. Observing others being beaten is likely to make children feel frightened and traumatized, which highlights the psychological side-effects of witnessing physical violence.

Children in the PRU often referred to physical violence as 'not bullying'. Overt violence was more common in the PRU than in the state schools and private school and became normalized. When Duncan had his teeth 'smashed' by another boy, John, he did not consider the violent act as bullying and neither did his peers, partly because they thought Duncan provoked John: 'they just knacked my teeth up, that's not bullying, that's just me being cheeky' (Duncan, Year 10, Priory Lane PRU). However, the fight between the boys had a significant impact on several other boys who eagerly told me about it as soon as they saw me, even though it had happened a week ago. 'There isn't bullying at this school, Duncan got banged last week. John knocked his teeth in…he deserved it; he's had it coming to him for ages' (Gavin, Year 10, Priory Lane PRU).

'Bystanders' and 'friends'

Luke felt inadvertently involved in ostracizing other pupils:

> Before I started the football team Mr Jackson would ignore me all the time and now he's always talking to me, some people get treated better than others… Everybody treats me better… Sometimes when they're by themselves you feel sorry for them when you're watching them and there's no one talking to 'em.
>
> (Luke, Year 7, Woodlands School)

Luke expressed sympathy for ostracized children, which challenges Sullivan, Cleary and Sullivan (2004) who argued that bystanders may be complacent or ignore consequences of their behaviour. Although Luke may appear to be a 'bystander' he expressed empathy and exercised his voice about how he received favourable treatment at the expense of other pupils. This highlights how children who observe bullying and do not appear to do anything can be more affected by bullying than is typically assumed and the construction of them as simply 'bystanders' is too simplistic. Luke felt coerced by his peers, teacher and school norms to reinforce the ostracism of his peers which restricted his agency. Interestingly, none of the children in this research referred to themselves as 'bystanders' who simply overlooked the bullying process.

Matthew felt coerced into playing a game where his 'friend' David, who is popular, whips him and other children:

> He found this piece of wood and he starts whipping everyone with it. It's turned into a bit of a game now because pretty much everyone plays it… I can see from this window, he's just walked past and everyone's running past him.
>
> (Matthew, Year 7, Highcross Private School)

Although Matthew felt annoyed with David's domination and control: 'I'm just fed up of him ruling everything', he is afraid that if he does not play the game he will be ostracized from his peer group: 'I don't want to go around at lunch-time with no one there.' In 'grey' areas in friendship groups where bullying *may* be present, power usually operates through more fluid and sophisticated means than the traditional approach considers.

Maria who had just moved to a new school felt ostracized by her 'friends':

> My teacher came into the classroom and said, 'Tell me when you stop arguing, girls, cos Tanya feels piggy in middle.' [I feel] left out; cos they always sit together and when I ask them if I can sit next to them, they're like, 'I'm sitting next to Emily.'
>
> (Maria, Year 6, Pennitown Primary School)

Maria said she felt 'angry' as a consequence of feeling ostracized, which may have contributed to her not wanting to affiliate with Emily: 'I don't want to sit on the same table as her.' However, Maria did not reflect on how her avoidance of Emily may have upset her and how Tanya felt torn. Power is fluid and dynamic as pupils appeared to take turns in excluding and upsetting each other. Maria's teacher considers the conflict as 'arguing' and expects the children to stop voluntarily. She does not investigate what underlying issues are contributing to the conflict or whether there is bullying. Maria believes the problems are impossible to resolve – 'it's never gonna be better' – and is grappling with unhealthy relationships in which she feels entrapped (Nassem 2017). She explains how her teacher is 'sick of it' and highlights how persistent unresolved conflicts and tensions between pupils can adversely affect both pupils and teachers.

Why Do Children Bully?

'To be popular'

Popularity was the main response to the question 'Why do children bully?' One answer which summed this up was 'To look better and be popular':

> I don't think popular people are good, they think they're better than everybody else...and people will like them because they're bullying somebody; they think it's good to bully people for attention...they get called 'slags' after because they're always hanging around with boys.
>
> (Nicole, Year 10, Parklane School)

Children who engage in bullying are not necessarily well liked but they can have high status with peers (Caravita *et al.* 2009). Nicole demonstrates a common finding about how popularity can achieve social gains (Jacobson 2010), such as influencing others – by 'telling you what to do' – and admiration – such as 'respect' and being 'cool' (Nassem 2017, p.295).

She also highlights a rare finding that enhanced visibility can subject children to bullying because of the exposure and attention that popularity can bring which limits the power that popular children have over peers. This finding expands previous research by Bansel *et al.* (2009) who found that positions of power can be changed by the peer group so someone who has social power over their peers can become targeted and victimized. Jealousy and resentment can develop towards those who have desirable attributes (such as social, academic or sporting success) and receive favourable treatment, for example from their peers and/or teachers as a consequence. Maria (Year 6, Pennitown Primary School) explains, 'I'm head girl and they're jealous because they wanted to be it, so I can't even mention head girl in front of them.'

Edward, like Matthew, was also whipped by popular children with sticks. He explains how popular children are usually approved of by pupils and teachers:

> The bullies think of ways to get to you... The person with the stick will say, 'Sit in the bin or I'll put you in the bin!' They look for sticks, find the longest one they could get and start hitting each other with it. One boy might decide to pick on you and have a stick...he'd hit you, then you'd run

and they'd just carry on hitting you. Cos they've been at school longest teachers like them, if I had the stick I'd throw it… That's where I got that bruise from, they really hurt.

(Edward, Year 7, Highcross Private School)

Edward was bullied by his friends as part of a 'game' and appears to consent to the 'game' which conceals his bullying. He explains how popular children who engage in bullying can be inadvertently supported and reinforced by teachers. Bullying which instils conformity to group norms is generally accepted and approved of, often by both teachers and pupils (Nassem 2017). These findings add depth to Frey (2005) who found that the maltreatment that 'obedient' children engage in is often undetected by teachers.

It was generally accepted that certain children who are identified as 'weird' by their peers such as 'geeks' were marginalized and bullied, particularly by children who were popular:

There's people who are weird and strange, people might call 'em 'geeks'…they're in one group and other people are in the other group. The popular people don't mix with the other ones…if they got something wrong they'd laugh their heads off but if someone popular got it wrong they wouldn't laugh.

(Kimberly, Year 7, Highcross Private School)

Kimberly considers herself as 'popular' and feels that she is reinforcing social norms rather than instigating bullying. She was favoured by her head of year who chose her to show me around for the day. I observed her actively ostracizing her 'friends' by running to 'avoid them'. Kimberly blames institutional divisions and her peers for the 'harsh' way 'geeks' are treated by popular children. 'Geeks' were constructed as the 'other' and dehumanized, as found by Sondergaard (2012). Laughing at and ostracizing 'geeks' and calling them names are forms of bullying and humiliation concealed by group norms. Children indicate they are not intentionally bullying; rather they are striving to achieve peer approval and status which can provide temporary protection from bullying. In the private school, bullying through coercion to instil conformity was more prevalent than overt violence. However, 'geeks' did not experience the systemic bullying of those who were not performing well.

'Cos they're bored'

A common explanation for why children engage in bullying is boredom:

> Peter: They should find something else to do instead of bullying people.
> Interviewer: Why do you think they do it?
> Peter: Because they get a laugh out of it.
> Interviewer: Why do you think they want a laugh?
> Peter: Cos they're bored.

> (Peter, Year 10, Parklane School)

Boredom was associated with disengagement and children's minds 'switching off':

> Interviewer: When we're bored what happens to our minds?
> Mason: It turns to jelly and we think about anything.
> Emily: It switches off.

> (Fourth focus group, Year 7, Woodlands School)

Boredom can restrict children's sense of agency and moral guidance to the extent that they can cause problems to achieve the control, stimulation and entertainment which boredom removes. 'When it's boring loads of people mess about and throw things' (Sophia, Year 7, Woodlands School).

'Because they're bullied'

Some children in the lowest stream felt resentment towards those in the highest streams because they were usually perceived as being favoured by teachers. Many children in the lowest streams felt marginalized and targeted, which perpetuated bullying. Jack was persistently in trouble for bullying. He has severe dyslexia and provides a candid account of his frustrations:

> Interviewer: Why does it bother you that they ['swots'] get treated better?
> Jack: Because everybody's same.
> Interviewer: What might you do to a 'swot' who annoys you?
> Jack: 'Call 'em a 'swot', donkey-nut their tie [put their tie around a bar so they are hurt when they pull away].

> (Jack, Year 8, Parklane School)

Responding aggressively to being treated unfairly was common in working-class boys; as Jack explained, '[you] can't be a swot, you might be beaten up'. A 'swot' was considered to be a child who was achieving highly academically and/or a child who was particularly conforming towards teachers and school rules. 'Swots' tended to be bullied because being obedient, on good terms with teachers and achieving highly can set pupils against their peers.

Jack is physically aggressive to children who 'joke' with him. He takes out his feelings on children who torment him by making comments to him such as 'ah, I've done mine [homework]'. Comments such as these upset him because he is struggling with his school work. He does not consider his behaviour as bullying because he feels provoked by their psychological bullying where he believes he is positioned by his teachers and peers as inferior.

Children from working-class backgrounds who had learning difficulties often felt targeted by their peers, teachers and the school system:

> They kicked me out for fighting... I got bullied in primary school. That's why I don't let no one bully me now. It was all way through primary school until Year 6 when I turned around and hit 'em...that's what got me into fighting.
>
> (Carl, Year 11, Priory Lane PRU)

Carl stopped children bullying him when he retaliated but became permanently excluded from school as a consequence. Responding aggressively to peers achieves power over them but brings punishment from teachers (Mac an Ghaill 1994). Several children at Priory Lane PRU had been permanently excluded from school for being physically violent. Carl does not consider his behaviour as bullying because the psychological bullying he has endured throughout school has contributed to his aggressive response. He was identified by teachers as the source of the problem and punished whilst children who bullied him were not reprimanded as teachers did not realize how he was victimized. Since being excluded Carl felt his personal circumstances had worsened. He said he was surrounded by 'shit stirrers' where 'no one respects anyone', which causes him to become angry and 'lose his temper' (Nassem 2017).

None of the children in this book identified themselves as 'bullies' as they explained the underlying reasons which contributed to their aggression. Children attributed their maltreatment to their peers, teachers or the school system and did not accept responsibility for their behaviour and the effect it had on others. In summary, usually children are motivated to engage in bullying to achieve desirable outcomes (such as status and to release their anger) and other people are inadvertently hurt along the way.

Now the research evidence has been discussed the following section will outline how, based on your enhanced understanding of pupils' experiences of bullying, you can effectively help them.

'Empathetic Understanding' to Understand and Resolve Bullying
Scoping the problem

Take time to understand pupils' perceptions and experiences of bullying so you can tailor your anti-bullying strategies to their specific needs. Facilitating discussion groups with pupils about bullying can help you learn about their experiences. You could hold these discussions in PSHE, circle time or in any other class where you feel it is suitable.

To allow children to exercise their voice it is important to ask open questions. It can also be helpful to have some follow-up questions to ask. Examples of questions to ask children include:

- What is bullying?
- How does it feel to be bullied?
- Is teasing bullying? When does teasing become bullying?
- Why do children bully?
- What experiences of bullying do children have in school?
- What experiences of cyberbullying do children have?
- What do other pupils do when there is bullying?
- What do school staff do about bullying?
- What do you think is unhelpful in tackling bullying?
- What do you think we should do about bullying?

Asking pupils questions about teasing and bullying will enhance your knowledge about ambiguous cases so you can develop more effective strategies to respond to them before they can cause significant distress and escalate.

The last three questions can help you reflect on your own strategies to combat bullying, and, from this, you might want to improve the way you respond to bullying and support colleagues to improve how they respond. If you have a classroom discussion about bullying it is important that it does not result in children being bullied because of particularly personal information that they have shared about their experiences. In a large discussion, such as in a classroom, avoid asking personal questions such as 'what experiences of bullying have you had?' If you feel children are sharing personal information which could make them susceptible to bullying then steer the conversation to more general discussions about bullying and speak with the child individually at the end of the session about their own personal experiences, ensuring that any additional support required for them is provided. If you do not feel it is appropriate to have discussions in class about bullying you could facilitate smaller group discussions, for example, with four to six pupils, which could be followed up by speaking with children individually if any serious concerns are raised.

To understand what children's experiences of school are like and how they experience boredom you could observe a class for the whole day in lessons, as they move between lessons and at break-times. When children say they are bored, ask them what boredom feels like and what makes them bored. When those who are being punished say they feel bored, it is particularly important to be vigilant because children can become disengaged and it can reduce children's morality becoming detached as their minds start 'switching off' which can increase their unacceptable behaviour and bullying. Bullying can provide entertainment, stimulation and a feeling of control which can mitigate boredom. Find out from children what they think could be done to help reduce their experience of boredom and consider with pupils and colleagues how some of the pupils' suggestions can be put into practice by staff.

Suspected cases of bullying

You may feel that a child in your class could be being bullied but be uncertain about this. In 'grey' areas such as these, speak to the child individually and ask them how they are getting along with other pupils. If you have noticed that they are being teased you could tell them that you have witnessed some banter in their peer group and would like to know what is happening and how they are feeling about it. If the pupil suggests that they are just joking with one another and that they are not being bullied encourage them to talk about interactions within this peer group and listen carefully to what they say. Ask them if any other pupils are finding these interactions upsetting. Arrange to have follow-up conversations with the pupil at a later date to investigate if the suspected bullying is still present and/or has escalated. Observe more closely how these children interact with each other in future. You could also speak to other pupils who are involved to find out what has happened and if bullying is present. This could provide an opportunity to ask these children, and the children who you teach, to consider how their interactions might constitute, and/or be perceived as, bullying.

Reported cases of bullying

When cases of bullying are reported to an appropriate member of staff (such as head of pastoral care, behaviour manager or head of year) then a member of staff can provide a series of meetings with the individuals involved in bullying. Meetings could firstly be on an individual basis and then the group involved could be brought together into discussions about what has happened and how to move forward. The 'empathetic understanding' approach will help you understand the underlying reasons which contribute to the bullying.

The priority should be to meet with those who are feeling victimized, have a meeting with them and listen to their experiences. In conversations with those who feel victimized ask them what happened, if there were witnesses, how they felt, when it started, how it started and who has been involved. There may be a longer history to the bullying than you first realized. Ask the pupil who is victimized what they want to be done about the bullying and how they want it to be dealt with. Discuss with the pupil the advantages and disadvantages of each suggested strategy, the most effective way to deal with the bullying, and agree how the bullying will be addressed. Through facilitating these discussions, you will work in partnership with children so you enhance both your understanding of their bullying and your understanding of what to do about it. You might not be able to deal with things exactly how the pupil wants you to, for example, a child who is severely bullied might not want you to do anything, which you should not do. However, involving the pupil who is victimized in the decision-making process means you can support them to have an active part in resolving their bullying.

After you have spoken to the child who is victimized it is important to speak with those who are engaging in the bullying. The child who is perceived as engaging in bullying is likely to be defensive, for example by blaming the victimized child and/or stating that they did not intend to cause harm because they 'didn't mean it' and/or they were 'only joking'. From meeting with the children involved in bullying you will learn more about their perspectives and motivations for engaging in bullying so you can deal with this more effectively. Explain that you are meeting with them to understand what has happened, resolve the conflict and understand why they behaved the way they did. Children who have engaged in bullying would benefit from the 'Mentoring for "Bullies" programme. 'Mentoring for "Bullies"' involves an adult mentor providing regular weekly meetings over approximately two months for those who persistently engage in bullying. It aims to enhance understanding of why these children are engaging in bullying, resolve these underlying issues, and improve how they respond to conflict. Through mentoring, schools can provide regular sessions to resolve bullying proactively, rather than just reacting to problematic behaviour after it has occurred.

Mentees are asked to explain recent incidents when they have had conflict with others to reflect on how their behaviour may have caused harm to other pupils and/or staff and learn how to behave more respectfully. You can role-play with mentees alternative ways they can respond to conflict to help them make more informed decisions about their behaviour. Explain to them why their behaviour is unacceptable. Clarify the choices they have made and likely consequences of the choices they make. Develop an individualized programme to show mentees how they can improve their behaviour.

Mentoring equips children with the necessary resources to respond to interactions and circumstances which cause them distress in more pro-social ways rather than engaging in bullying. This approach can reduce bullying without an over-reliance on overt punishment. It is more likely to contribute to more positive behaviour rather than sitting for hours in detention or isolation.

Children who have previously engaged in bullying, but who have learnt to refrain from doing so, can become positive role-models to other children, showing them how they can denounce their negative behaviour and preconceived ideas people have of them through transforming themselves. They can become anti-bullying advocates who help children learn how to refrain from bullying and gain status from their peers through more respectful behaviours. This process enables reformed pupils to perceive themselves more positively, and enables other staff and pupils to do so. It also provides a supportive network for children to learn from their peers how to exercise their agency in ways that benefit themselves and other pupils.

After speaking with the child (or children) who feels victimized and the child (or children) involved in the bullying individually about what happened, prepare for them to have a supervised conversation with each other about the bullying. However, ensure that the children feel comfortable enough to have the meeting and that you feel it could be beneficial for them. In the first instance the victimized child is likely to feel frightened of being in a room with just the person that bullies them and another adult. Ideally, facilitate several pre-meetings with individuals to prepare and support them to meet with each other. If there is significant conflict between these children, which may have been present for several years, then you could facilitate a series of meetings with these children, for example, three or four meetings over a month.

In these meetings, explain the importance of being honest throughout this process so that effective resolutions can be made, and remind them of their agreement with you if they start to be dishonest. If children are persistently dishonest you could explain that more intensive strategies may need to be implemented if you cannot resolve the matter through open and reflective dialogue. This may involve working more closely with the mentee, colleagues and parents to reflect upon why support is not effective and consider other strategies to encourage the mentee to be more open and reflective. Additional forms of support could involve mentees attending a retreat. Children can attend retreats for a day, or retreats could be provided for several days for mentees to attend instead of their usual classes to enable them to participate in a more intensive programme to address their behaviour and learn how to improve. On retreat, children will be supported to reflect more deeply about their behaviour and learn more about the perspectives of others. They will be supported to have more intensive dialogue with other pupils, staff and their parents about what is causing their behaviour and understand the impact of their actions on others.

Through mediating with individuals who are in conflict, you can enhance their understanding of each other's perspectives so you can work together to find a resolution. Perhaps you could ask children to reflect upon what they think would be helpful in resolving existing conflict and tensions after the session has been held; they can then discuss these points in following meetings. Ensure you speak to the people who are more broadly involved in the bullying to understand the problem and what happened. Involve these children in developing and implementing strategies to resolve the bullying and ensure they have an input. Throughout this process, listen carefully to what has happened, how individuals feel and what has contributed to their hurt feelings. To help children find workable solutions to their bullying, collaborate with colleagues, as well as pupils, to develop the most effective strategies to resolve the bullying.

Establish an anti-bullying advisory group for colleagues (staff ABAG) to meet regularly to discuss issues of bullying and share strategies to overcome it. A pupils' anti-bullying advisory group (pupil ABAG), where pupils meet regularly to discuss issues of bullying and share strategies to overcome it, could also feed into the staff ABAG. The pupil and staff ABAG should consist of a core team who meet regularly to understand more about bullying and develop effective strategies to tackle it. The ABAGs can enhance the connectivity of peers and colleagues which has been cited as one of the benefits of pupil-led approaches (Leat, Reid and Lofthouse 2015). The pupil and staff ABAG could have a central role in enhancing knowledge about children's experiences of bullying in their school and developing strategies to resolve it. The pupil and staff ABAG could consist of a group of children and staff who volunteer to regularly attend and contribute to the meetings and follow up with the actions developed by the group, for example, future research and development of school policies such as managing bullying. To encourage a safe space for pupils and staff to talk, pupils and staff should usually meet separately so there will be both a pupil and a staff ABAG. Although it is important that the staff and pupils meet separately to discuss their specific issues, in addition they could also hold a series of joint staff and pupil ABAG meetings to work together to address their shared concerns of bullying. This can strengthen the resources of pupils and teachers to collaboratively resolve bullying. As soon as you have established a pupil and staff ABAG, meet with pupils, staff (including teachers, support staff such as teaching assistants and lunch-time supervisors) and parents to inform your school community about the work you are doing so they can actively engage with it from the beginning. This can contribute to a wider engagement from your school in implementing an anti-bullying culture. The pupil and staff ABAG could be led by the head of pastoral care who feeds back the knowledge gained and recommendations of how to resolve the bullying to the school's headteacher, or deputy head, and senior management team.

'Take Responsibility'

The original finding in my research that none of the children considered themselves as bullies highlights that children are not realizing the negative effects their behaviour can have on others. Rather than reflecting on the hurt children have caused to others, they focus primarily on their own hurt. Through 'take responsibility', children are encouraged to critically reflect on how their behaviour may make others feel and learn how they can exercise their agency more respectfully. To implement this approach, teach pupils how they can be inadvertently involved in hurting others. Become more alert to children's inadvertent comments and behaviours and have strategies in place to resolve this. An offensive comment made in class could be used to stimulate discussion on how recipients and observers of this behaviour might feel and react as a consequence, and why this might happen. Explain how behaviours which may be unintentional can still cause harm, and provide a classroom session on bullying and teasing. Since bullying is normalized, ensure that you openly discuss hurtful comments that children say without publicly targeting those who make the comments. However, if seriously offensive comments have been made then speak with those involved individually and/or in smaller groups. Classroom discussions could involve topics such as how pupils can be inadvertently involved in hurting others, for example leaving them out. Ask pupils: how do we ensure we realize when we are hurting others? What can we do as an individual, class and school to help individuals who we hurt, or who are hurt by others? Children's views and feedback could contribute to developing and enhancing the school's anti-bullying policy.

The Department for Education (2017) advises schools to openly discuss difference and explain that prejudice-based language is not accepted. To illustrate your points, draw on real-life examples. I have been informed of an incident which happened in the workplace where an employee, Emma, referred to her computer as being 'so gay', which offended her colleague who made a formal complaint about her. Emma's comment was investigated by her manager and she explained how casually referring to objects as 'gay' had become normal to her as 'everyone had said it in school'. Through her behaviour being investigated, Emma realized how offensive her flippant remark was and how it constituted offensive homophobic language. She made a public apology online to all the people she might have hurt as a consequence. Her experience highlights how important it is for children to learn the legal consequences that engaging in discrimination, such as casual homophobic language, can have on their lives and those of others such as in the workplace.

To encourage children to stop focusing only on their own victimization and reflect on the effects their behaviour has on others you could work with small groups of about five pupils in a more confidential setting over several weeks. Ask children to share their experiences of bullying and then provide examples of when they may have engaged in these behaviours towards others. Consider why the individuals behaved the way they did and what impact their own behaviour was likely to have had on the situation. Through role-play you can act out what happened to illustrate the issues. One child could express how the perpetrator felt and explain why they behaved the way they did, and another child could discuss the feelings and rationale behind the behaviour of those victimized. In addition, consider (and possibly demonstrate through role-play) alternative ways individuals could have behaved and likely consequences of these behaviours.

To support pupils to be responsible when they are communicating online, for example, in the information they post, and how they respond to others, speak to children about the following matters: what issues they have experienced through online communication; what cyberbullying means to them; how individuals have communicated with others in ways that could be perceived as cyberbullying; and if they have any ideas about how to deal with cyberbullying. This information can be generated from classroom sessions or with focus groups with about five individuals in each group.

To encourage children to articulate their voice, and draw upon their experiences to resolve bullying, consult with them about your school's anti-bullying policy. Perhaps children could contribute to updating and even writing/revising your school's anti-bullying policy. You can use examples from children of the bullying and cyberbullying they have experienced to help you clarify behaviours which constitute bullying in your policy. Within your school's anti-bullying policy explain how your school will listen to, and act on, the child's voice, for example, through facilitating pupil-led anti-bullying campaigns. You could facilitate a politically active project on bullying through which children learn about what the government advises should be done about bullying, for example by referring to guidelines on bullying from the Department for Education regarding how bullying should be tackled, and asking whether children feel that there is anything else in this which should be developed, added or challenged. Following this research, compile letters from your students, which you can then use to write a collective letter to send to the local MP of your school. From this, you may want to write a charter or code of good practice with pupils and colleagues to help understand and deal with bullying.

'Healthy Relationships Between Pupils'
Bullying is normalized

Characteristics of bullying and 'grey' areas such as name-calling and teasing which may not necessarily cause visible signs of distress are enmeshed within pupils' everyday experiences of school. Olweus' (1993) definition is limited in addressing children's mundane and 'grey' experiences of bullying. In five out of the six secondary state school focus groups, bullying was evident which mainly consisted of name-calling (of names such as 'scrubber') and teasing, for example, 'we call him Rocky cos he never wins' (fifth focus group, Year 7, Northfield School):

> Interviewer: Does anyone here not call people names?
>
> Jake: Yeah, me and Ollie.
>
> Chelsea: I don't say it often; you call him (Craig) 'pees over there'.
>
> Sam: Only about four seconds ago.
>
> Interviewer: Can we imagine school without this?
>
> Louis and Claire: No.
>
> Max: You can't imagine school like that.
>
> Sam: It'd be a lot nicer.
>
> Louis: It'd be too formal, it would have all the kids asleep.
>
> Jake: That's natural for a school, everyone does it.
>
> (Fourth focus group, Year 7, Woodlands School)

'Grey' areas which are prevalent in children's daily interactions are perceived by them as fundamental to school and are generally accepted. In the quotation previously presented, the teasing of Craig involved several of his peers – 'everybody kept taking the mick out of me' – which 'annoyed' him. However, there were individual differences as children such as Sam, who was also present in the focus group, did not normalize bullying. Craig appears to be experiencing mild bullying which makes him feel slightly angry and irritated although there may be more serious bullying beneath the surface (Nassem 2017).

Implementation of the 'healthy relationships' approach

The 'healthy relationships' approach can encourage pupils to develop respectful social interactions and challenge normalized practices which enable bullying. Facilitate classroom discussions about what behaviours may appear to be accepted but which can cause significant harm. Ask children how they can respectfully respond to behaviours which they consider to be harmful or abusive. Discuss bullying that can exist within friendship groups, between pupils and teachers, and bullying which is not reported or witnessed by teachers in this discussion. Don't dismiss reports of bullying between friends, even if they appear to make up later. You might not consider the conflict between friends as clearly bullying but they might be enmeshed within abusive relationships which can be harmful and need to be addressed. Find out what these children are saying and doing to each other to learn how you can help them interact with each other more respectfully.

Children who accept abusive relationships and behaviours as normal may continue to accept them in their social and interpersonal relationships as adults and so they can become entrenched in their lives. Ask children what healthy relationships look and feel like, how we can realize when people are hurting us and what we can do about this. Support children to develop strategies so they can respectfully challenge relationships which may have become abusive. In classroom discussion ask children to write examples on the board and discuss what behaviours are unacceptable from others and what we should do when we experience these behaviours. Children could be encouraged to consider how they can defend themselves from bullying in ways that are respectful to others and not become abusive. Furthermore, you might want to embed some of the children's suggestions into a 'healthy relationships' policy or a 'healthy relationships' part of your anti-bullying policy to maximize their input. Encourage children to make friends with other people outside of their traditional friendship circle to enhance their support network and social skills. However, some children might find this difficult if they want to be accepted within the friendship group which is bullying them; for example, children who want to be popular may primarily want to be part of the popular group.

For children to have healthy relationships with their peers it is of paramount importance that they develop a healthy relationship with themselves. Encouraging children to accept themselves and improve their self-esteem is likely to help them develop an internal self-worth so they are not constantly striving for social approval from their peer group or feel resentful to individuals who have characteristics which they desire. Supporting children to develop their psychological strength can reduce their likelihood of being negatively influenced by others and engaging in bullying. Throughout this process children can overcome their fears of being ostracized and help others who are bullied.

Work with children in small groups to find out how they perceive themselves, and encourage them to question any negative perceptions they have of themselves to develop a healthier identity. They can question these perceptions both internally by improving how they perceive themselves and externally by respectfully challenging those who hurt them. An example of how I implemented this work is provided in Chapter 7 which discusses the pupil-led anti-bullying intervention. By challenging children's negative comments about themselves and others, and listening to and responding to children's views about bullying, you can help combat the various forms of bullying which they might experience throughout their school day.

Provide children with a diary and encourage them to record their interactions with other pupils and school staff, and how they feel. Encourage them to write in their diary regularly, for example, every day they are at school. Diaries can help provide a positive outlet for children's emotions and encourage them to critically reflect upon how they respond to others. A paper diary will be sufficient but you may want to set up an online diary for children as long as it is confidential. Ask children if they want to show you their diaries to increase your knowledge of their everyday experiences, interactions, thoughts, feelings and responses. You may want to discuss with pupils in small confidential groups what interactions they have recorded in their diary and critically discuss how they can respond effectively to their bullying. Support children to individually or collectively write a fictional story about bullying based on their experiences which they may have diarized, and discuss how it can be resolved. Reflect with children about which strategies are most likely to be the most effective and include these in their story. This book could become an anti-bullying resource for the school which other children and staff can read, discuss and reflect upon.

Conclusion

Children's perceptions and experiences of bullying have been examined. The most common reasons why children engage in bullying have been discussed and the complexity of children's involvement in bullying has been analyzed. Recommendations have been provided of how you can support children to understand the perspectives of other children more, take responsibility for the effects their behaviour has on others, and develop healthier relationships with themselves and their peers. How you can thoroughly investigate bullying and deal with the underlying reasons why children engage in bullying has also been outlined.

Chapter 3

Empowering School Practitioners to Resolve Bullying

This chapter examines the complex positioning of how school practitioners are situated in school to respond to bullying. It includes practitioners who feel victimized by pupils, those who are sometimes perceived as 'picking on' pupils, and those who are unsure of how to deal with school bullying. The strategy 'empowering practitioners' is discussed; this explains how practitioners can strengthen their position in school and enhance their support to deal with bullying authoritatively. The 'healthy relationships' approach is expanded to include ways pupils and teachers can develop more respectful ways of perceiving and interacting with each other. The 'empathetic understanding' model is also developed to encourage pupils and teachers to enhance their understanding of one another's position and perspective. Advice on how bullying between pupils and teachers can be incorporated into anti-bullying policies is also outlined.

Recommendations by the Department for Education

Schools and teachers have a legal responsibility to protect children from bullying and tackle bullying when it occurs. In *Preventing and Tackling Bullying: Advice for Headteachers, Staff and Governing Bodies*, the Department for Education (2017) highlights the legal duty of schools to have measures in place to prevent bullying. Schools will not be marked down by Ofsted for having bullying; instead Ofsted focus on how bullying has been resolved. Schools should make it easy for pupils to report bullying, and ensure that pupils are made aware of how they can prevent bullying. Parents should also have awareness of school procedures for dealing with bullying and feel confident to report it.

The Department for Education (2017) advises schools to work with the wider community such as the police so their expertise can have an input into dealing with bullying. It states that disciplinary measures should be used for pupils who engage in bullying in order to show clearly that the behaviour is wrong, and these procedures should be applied fairly and consistently. When there is a 'reasonable cause to suspect that a child is suffering, or is likely to suffer significant harm' (p.6) through a bullying incident it should be addressed as a child protection concern under the Children Act 1989.

These guidelines appear to be clear and concise; however, in practice it is not so straightforward. For example, how do you distinguish between harm and significant harm? Parents who do not speak the same language as most of the other pupils and staff in school may be less aware of your school's procedures and feel less confident reporting bullying. Your school may not have developed a strong network of external agencies which can make it difficult for you to work with the wider community. In this chapter, strategies are provided to help you overcome issues such as these and deal with the complex cases of bullying you are likely to be confronted with throughout your career.

The Role of Teachers in School Bullying

Although bullying is often hidden from teachers, there are many 'grey' areas of bullying which are often prevalent in the classroom. 'Grey' areas include characteristics associated with bullying such as name-calling, hitting and kicking which may not do the following: cause visible stress to individuals, involve a clear imbalance of power, or be repeated, or intentional. Bullying which occurs in front of teachers often consists of overt name-calling, for example, some children are called 'thick' in class by their peers, and ostracism where one child might refuse to sit next to a certain child. These forms of bullying may appear to school practitioners as minor disagreements between friends and not bullying. However, even bullying which appears to be mild or a 'grey' area needs to be addressed; otherwise it can cause serious harm. Understandably, it is difficult for you to resolve bullying if you do not observe bullying and it is not reported to you. Furthermore, there are many cases of bullying which are not reported to staff. Methods for supporting pupils when bullying is reported and when it is not reported have been discussed in the previous chapter.

The Complex Positioning of School Practitioners
Punishments

Your power to resolve bullying is influenced by your position in school as you are obliged to follow school policies and procedures. This is likely to restrict your ability to make significant changes to how bullying is dealt with in your school. From the child's perspective, teachers typically respond to bullying through punishing 'bullies'. Punishments often involve teachers shouting at pupils, detentions, being put in isolation, and temporary or permanent exclusion from school.

Instead of improving behaviour and encouraging children to become more mindful of its impact on others, punitive methods often create more anger and resentment in children. Max (Year 10, Priory Lane PRU) reflects on the punishments he experienced, 'all detentions I had, they were all piss taking bastards'. Pupils frequently punished often do not understand what they have done wrong; in some cases, they also try to avoid being punished and can refuse to attend their detention:

> Sophia: If somebody came in actually and really told them 'what are you actually trying to achieve here?' they would have a second thought.
>
> Interviewer: Don't you think people do?
>
> Sophia and Natalie: No.
>
> Alice: They just give 'em lines.
>
> Natalie: Sometimes when you've been naughty they give you a detention and they won't tell you what you've done wrong.
>
> Isabelle: They don't really care they just go, 'oh, I'm not going to that detention'.
>
> Natalie: You get used to getting detentions and then they don't say what you're doing wrong, so they don't stop. But when they say right, you've done this, if you're actually talking to somebody one-to-one they'll actually listen.
>
> Reece: They give red cards and yellow cards like medals.
>
> (Tenth focus group, Year 7, Highcross Private School)

Children usually do not feel their punishments are applied fairly and consistently, as the Department for Education (2017) have advised they should be. In the focus group which has just been presented, children suggested that rather than overt punishments, staff should encourage children to reflect on what they have done. They imply that when interventions focus on talking to children about their behaviour and encouraging them to think about its effects, it is likely to improve.

Alternatively, children who are frequently punished can become accustomed, and hardened, to the punishments so they are no longer upset by them. Reece, in the quotation just presented, highlights how children who are punished can achieve social rewards and status from their peers such as respect, attention and recognition as a consequence of misbehaving. This is partly because children are challenging traditional forms of power which operate over them, including the position of teachers who generally have more power than them.

Bullied for 'grassing'

Overtly punishing children who engage in bullying rarely stops bullying; in some cases bullying temporarily stops, but then continues. Many children said that when they reported bullying to teachers it escalated as a consequence and they were subsequently bullied even more for 'grassing'. Over-reliance on interventions which use overt punishment can increase the anger of 'bullies' which they can subsequently take out on the pupils they target. This vicious cycle was frequently experienced by victimized children. For example, Shaun (Year 8, Townville School) explained, 'I told teacher and then that lad come back and hit me because he says I'm a wus':

> Marcus: When teachers say 'you can tell us anything'.
> Liam: For bullying if you tell a teacher.
> Edwina: They don't do anything.
> Liam: You just get bullied even more then.
> Marcus: And if you told, you get called a grasser.
>
> (Ninth focus group, Year 7, Highcross Private School)

Children often felt they could not get help from teachers to resolve their bullying, although many did not report it to them. Bullying tends to be of a persistent nature and usually happens every day they are at school, for example, 'the stick thing [getting whipped by boys with a stick] doesn't happen daily, but something will happen daily' (Edward, Year 7, Highcross Private School).

Children usually felt helpless in dealing with their maltreatment and felt entrapped. Some pupils felt that teachers punished them for being bullied, for example, by excluding them from class when they were trying to defend themselves. These children subsequently felt 'picked on' by their teachers for being bullied:

Peter: I've been excluded quite a few times, because I've walked out of isolation because it wasn't my fault, so I felt that I shouldn't have been punished.

Interviewer: What do you think the teachers can do about the bullying?

Peter: They can put them in isolation and not me for sticking up for myself.

(Peter, Year 10, Parklane School)

Abstract Messages

Formal teaching and learning about bullying tended to be presented by teachers in abstract ways which did not fully address children's personal experiences of bullying. In the following quotation pupils explain how their teacher used drama where they participated in a play of a 'fictional' event about bullying. Children said this play helped them understand how it feels to be bullied:

Jake: Miss Smith teaches Drama and when we had that bullying day she was helping us, telling us not to bully.

Sam: We did an activity, Jason knows how it feels to be called names, he was pretending to be the boy that got bullied by his dad. We were playing a game, then he walked in and everybody gave him a dirty look.

Sam: And call him bad things.

Chelsea: She put it in a way to let us know how it feels.

Jake: When he [Mason, a participant of this focus group] came to this school people were like that to him at first.

(Fourth focus group, Year 7, Woodlands School)

After children had participated in this play, they recognized how a boy in the focus group, Mason, had been bullied when he first joined the school. However, they did not reflect on their current behaviour, which has been presented in the previous chapter (in the 'Bullying is normalized' section) where children in this focus group tormented another boy by saying several times that he 'pees in the bath'. When bullying is taught in an abstract way, for example, about fictional characters and scenarios developed by adults, children may reflect on their past behaviour and display empathy towards these characters. However, they may not necessarily consider how their current behaviour can be construed as bullying.

Listening to Pupils

Catherine suggests that often teachers do not listen, intervene to stop bullying, or take the maltreatment and harmful side-effects seriously enough:

> I've told plenty of teachers when my friends have been bullied and that's why there's so much fighting cos they do not listen and school is a nasty place. I remember going to high school and somebody would say 'I'm after you' and I'd be absolutely petrified so I'd go and tell teachers and they'd do nothing, they'd stick us in the same lesson… If they knew how my little sister is petrified at 11 years old to walk to her primary school, they [teachers] don't realize how it's affecting people inside, I don't think they take it in as much.
>
> (Catherine, Year 11, Priory Lane PRU)

Catherine indicates that there is a dichotomy between children's experiences of bullying and what teachers understand bullying to be. She also indicates that children's needs for safety and protection from bullying are usually ignored and dismissed by teachers who do not adequately safeguard victims from bullying. Instead, she indicates that teachers simply carry on as normal. Jack, like most other children, feels his voice is oppressed in school:

> You can't give your own opinions; you can't talk to 'em [teachers], they always talk down to you and you have to talk to them. It's like they're queen and you're just a normal person out on street, got to bow down to 'em.
>
> (Jack, Year 7, Parklane School)

Jack believes that there is a hierarchy in school where teachers are at the highest point and he is at the bottom part. He does not feel a sense of belonging or acceptance and he feels violated that he is expected to worship his teachers.

Although Catherine (Year 11, Priory Lane PRU) was generally critical of teacher intervention (in her previous quotation) when there was bullying, she also had a positive experience in the PRU she attended where her teachers listened to her. She explains, 'Once I told Kate [teacher] that was it, Brian [head-teacher] and everybody listened and it stopped.' Catherine highlights how intervention can be successful when teachers take the issues which children raise seriously, pay attention to what children are saying and work together with colleagues to resolve the matter.

A minority of children felt their teachers were helpful in resolving their conflicts with other pupils: 'We've got Miss Booth and Miss Lee so if there are any fights in class Miss Booth can sort it out.' However, in these cases bullying tended to be overt and physical. Teachers can be more reluctant to intervene when bullying is psychological, social/relational and involves 'grey' areas rather than overt bullying.

The Influence of the School Environment on Teachers

There was quite a high level of disruption in all the schools in which I conducted observations, although it was particularly prevalent in the lower streams of the state school and the PRU. Jack (Year 7, Parklane School) describes what his school looks like: 'kids messing about, chewing gum all over, staff shouting, people running about'. He indicates that, in his school, pupils are disobedient, and staff lack control and react aggressively towards pupils. An environment where there is a high level of disruption and disorder is likely to undermine the authority of teachers and makes it difficult for them to manage their class which restricts their ability and power to handle bullying effectively.

A high level of disruption adversely influenced children's learning because, as one child reported, 'you can't concentrate right' which can distract and unsettle them. However, in the private school, some children also felt dissatisfied and distracted by the disruption in their class. 'It annoys me because the teachers have to keep telling 'em to stop…and then the teacher just shouts at them and it makes me jump' (Natasha, Year 7, Highcross Private School).

Behaviour management in school usually involved teachers issuing warnings and detentions to children when they misbehaved. School punishment is usually based on a hierarchical model where punishment is gradual and linear as one form of sanction tends to occur before the other and sanctions become progressively more severe (Foucault 1979):

I observe the notice-board behind Mr Stuart's desk and there are notices of rules, rewards and sanctions. On Mr Stuart's desk there are green behaviour slips to sign. There is a pyramid-shaped hierarchy of how to control pupils' behaviour, for example, first warning, second warning.

(Observation, Northfield School)

These practices which aim to manage children's behaviour can increasingly target children identified as misbehaving, as Grant (Year 11, Priory Lane PRU) explains, 'You get three comments and you get a detention and then it just adds up, I just think they're trying to getting you kicked out.'

Children who are identified as misbehaving feel increasingly 'picked on' by their teachers which usually leads to further punishments. These findings support Hepburn (1997) who argues that teacher–pupil relationships revolve around teachers bullying pupils who are identified by them as misbehaving. She found their 'bad behaviour' was recorded and led to them being punished whilst the misbehaviour of other pupils was not.

Bullying between Teachers and Pupils
Children feeling 'picked on' by teachers

Some children said they were unfairly 'picked on' and unjustly punished by teachers for: forgetting a pen, not reading out loud in class when they have dyslexia, being the only one in class who was not rewarded, or being told that their performance in PE was 'rubbish'. Children felt it was fairly common that they were shouted at by teachers and some were distressed by this: 'When you do something, you get shouted at and it makes you hurt and you start to cry' (Mila, Year 7, Woodlands School). When children felt distressed by these experiences with their teachers they were considered as on a spectrum of bullying. However, in instances where children did not appear to be upset by these behaviours then it was considered as a 'grey' area.

There were children who retaliated when they were shouted at by teachers, which implies that shouting at children is not necessarily a useful way to control the class. 'Most of the class do shout back at him when he shouts at them because he doesn't shout in a nice way, he's really shouting' (Stephanie, Year 10, Parklane School). Stephanie indicates that her teacher's shouting is aggressive, extreme and unpleasant.

Grant explains how children who are frequently involved in conflict with their teachers can respond aggressively to them because they feel provoked:

> Grant: I don't like people shouting at me. Why shout when you can talk to me?
> Interviewer: What might you do when people shout at you?

Grant: Kick off, start swearing and chucking stuff…you can't win against a teacher. They've always got to be right. If you say something to them, if they've got something in their head, that's that, you've done it, and if you do they start going leet and then I go leet.

(Grant, Year 11, Priory Lane PRU)

'Leet' refers to being wild and aggressive. Children who resisted their teachers' authority by retaliating aggressively reinforced their feelings of being 'picked on' by teachers. Grant felt his teacher abused his power over him by shouting. Grant shows how bullying between pupils and teachers can be associated with children retaliating aggressively because they feel they cannot exercise their voice (Nassem 2017). He became permanently excluded from school because of his behaviour which highlights how restricted his power and voice was.

Children bullying their teachers

In some cases, teachers who appeared to be vulnerable, for example, 'soft' teachers were bullied by pupils. Catherine explains how several pupils took pleasure in bullying their teacher when she could not manage her class. 'If teacher was a pushover then that was it; that was just one of the best lessons, she just got it for the rest of the year' (Catherine, Year 11, Priory Lane PRU). There was a higher level of conflict and hostility between teachers and pupils in the lower streams and PRU:

Holly and Anna: I feel thick.
Danni: I'm thick, teachers are harder on us and take things out on us…
Anna: I hate teachers.
Sally: Bridgette's not nice now she shouts at teachers; she calls Mr Morris Spit-nose.
Anna: Cos he's gay, he shouts at you for getting your planner out.
John: He gives you late marks for coming 20 seconds late.

(Fifth focus group, Year 7, Northfield School)

Children who felt marginalized by the education system and provoked by teachers sometimes bullied them in retaliation. If teachers are victimized by pupils their ability to support pupils who are bullied becomes restricted. However, in the private school, teachers were more respected and spoken about favourably. Steven, who was in Year 7 at the private school, reported, 'All the teachers are great.'

Statements children make such as 'strict teachers control their class' and 'children do not behave for soft teachers' place teachers in a position where they are required to exercise their power. Although 'strict teachers' are perceived as being able to manage their class effectively they can also be perceived as 'picking on' children and abusing their power. This places teachers in a difficult position and highlights how they are expected to use their authority to control pupils yet, conversely, this control can be construed as bullying. Furthermore, teachers are expected to encourage children to learn which often involves highlighting areas for development in children which can be perceived as pointing out their deficits. Consequently, pupils may feel upset and/or angry and take their anger out on staff. Findings have demonstrated the importance of teachers being firm towards pupils but not aggressive towards pupils. When pupils are disruptive and teachers are under pressure to ensure children are performing at the required academic standards, using power productively can be a difficult balance to negotiate.

Strategies for School Practitioners to Resolve Bullying
Bullying and 'healthy relationships' between educators and pupils

Developing 'healthy relationships' in school so pupils and school practitioners interact with one another with respect is likely to reduce bullying between them and reduce feelings of victimization. To lead by example, it is important that school practitioners speak to children respectfully all the time. You can improve your relationships with pupils by listening to them, taking time to understand their perspectives and respectfully responding to their views. Pupils are then more likely to do the same with their peers. There is a great deal of pressure on staff to ensure children are achieving academically; this can have an adverse impact on pupils who are struggling with their work who can feel marginalized. Reflect on how you respond to children who are having difficulties with their studies. Be aware of the significant impact your behaviour and language may have on these children as they can be susceptible to being bullied by pupils and other teachers.

It can be difficult for teachers to deal with conflict in their class and inequalities that they have not caused; for example, children may have learnt to be aggressive towards others from their families. To help you manage problems such as these you may want to learn more about how external factors associated with school can negatively influence how pupils interact with their peers and teachers. Some school practitioners may have developed unconscious habits and behaviours which may inadvertently contribute to bullying; for example, consider how you inform pupils that their work is not at the required standard. Discuss with colleagues and pupils how you can instil a sense of belonging in school for pupils from all backgrounds.

To help resolve conflict between a pupil and a teacher, a senior member of staff could meet with the pupil and teacher separately to find out what the problems are and then bring them together into a meeting to talk about the issue and what to do about it. If a pupil is persistently engaging in bullying a member of staff then they could participate in the 'Mentoring for "Bullies"' programme to help reduce their maltreatment and improve their behaviour. Alternatively, if a member of staff is bullying a pupil then they may benefit from being a mentee on the 'Mentoring for "Bullies"' programme which can be facilitated by a more senior member of staff. In more severe cases of staff bullying pupils then you will need to deal with this through your school's disciplinary procedure.

Your school would do well to introduce mandatory training on school bullying (which is updated regularly), and include the topic of understanding and resolving bullying between educators and pupils. Such training could also include strategies on dealing with bullying between educators and parents, and external visitors and parents. This can empower practitioners by supporting them to feel confident and equipped to deal with the various forms of bullying they may encounter.

'Empathetic understanding' between staff and pupils

If children have misbehaved, ensure you explain to them what they have done wrong and help them reflect upon the negative effect their behaviour has on other pupils and colleagues. This is a thought-provoking technique which encourages children to realize the harm their behaviour causes. The 'empathetic understanding' strategy is expanded here to encourage pupils and teachers to enhance their understanding of one another's position and perspective. To encourage staff and pupils to work together to tackle bullying, hold joint meetings and discussions for staff and pupils about bullying and what to do about it. Ask staff and children to volunteer to be part of an anti-bullying initiative and have several meetings with these pupils and staff to design, implement and evaluate a pupil-led approach to dealing with bullying. This pupil-led approach will provide pupils with a central role in advocating an anti-bullying culture.

Meetings between staff and pupils must be chaired effectively so that pupils and staff can work co-operatively on the group's goals to tackle bullying. These meetings provide a vehicle for different perspectives to be expressed, understood, reflected and acted upon. Through this dialogue, practitioners learn about children's perspective and children learn about adults' perspectives.

In these meetings about bullying between staff and pupils, individuals can share their concerns about bullying. Children may express that they feel that teachers ignore bullying. If children express this concern, discuss with them why they feel like this and how you can work with colleagues and pupils to do more about bullying. Support children to be involved in making decisions about how their bullying is dealt with. This will ensure children are listened to and that their recommendations are acted upon. Work with children to find out what incidents occurred prior to the incident they have reported and explore why pupils are engaging in bullying. Emphasize the importance of both teachers and pupils working together to make positive changes. By asking children about their experiences of bullying and feelings as a consequence of their bullying you will be more likely to identify when children are experiencing significant harm.

Developing interventions and campaigns which deal with children's lived experiences is likely to make more meaningful changes to their behaviour and lives rather than focusing on bullying which involves purely fictional characters. Have open dialogue with children about the behaviours which are associated with bullying but may not automatically be considered as bullying such as teasing. This can help you work with pupils to resolve these issues and nip bullying in the bud.

Help children understand your perspective as a school practitioner; for example, explain what it is like for you when pupils are disruptive and how you are required to deal with their behaviour in your school. From this they will understand why they have been reprimanded for their behaviour. Once you have learnt about children's experiences of bullying reflect with them and your colleagues about how you can improve how bullying is dealt with in your school. If teachers think they deal effectively with bullying and children express that more could be done, reflect on why this is the case and what can be done to address these different perspectives.

Children have explained in this chapter that they want teachers to take bullying more seriously. If, after speaking with children, bullying appears to be more of a problem than you initially expected consider how you can create more support to deal with bullying and for it to be a higher priority, for example having a specific role for a member of staff to deal entirely with bullying. If you already have an individual person responsible for bullying but they have lots of other duties you could meet with colleagues and senior school managers to discuss with colleagues how to support them to have more time to deal specifically with bullying. They could provide drop-in sessions and pre-arranged appointments for children to meet with them to discuss their experiences of bullying so you can start to resolve the problem.

In the previous section, Catherine explained that there were times when pupils reported bullying to teachers and they did nothing. She had to sit in the same lessons as the people who bullied her which paralysed her with terror. Her experience highlights the importance of teachers seriously considering what resources they have available to make reasonable adjustments to support children who are bullied. Imagine what it is like having to sit next to the person who bullies you every day you are at work. Consider that there is also another place you could work comfortably without having to be in such close proximity to your perpetrator. If there is bullying between children who are in the same class causing them particular distress then it may be beneficial for them to be taught in separate classes, if only temporarily, until the problem can be resolved. There needs to be careful consideration about children moving classes because of bullying, and children should be involved and supported throughout this transition. The focus should be on resolving the conflict peacefully rather than punishing individuals. Although children who are separated from one another in class are likely to see each other in the playground, reducing their contact with one another could lessen their feelings of entrapment and the intensity of the conflict.

To support children throughout their transition of moving classes you could meet with them individually to talk about the process. Once conflicts have been resolved, and if you think it would be beneficial to them, you can arrange for the children to sit in the same lessons together again. Before you arrange for children to sit in the same class again, bring them into meetings together so they can share their feelings, discuss the problems they are having with each other and agree how they will move forward. This cycle of having meetings to express emotions, discuss conflict and agree how to proceed more respectfully in future is a strategy recommended throughout this book and can be referred to as 'development meetings'.

If a pupil shouts at you, respond calmly to help defuse the situation. Children may tell you that they are retaliating towards their teachers because they feel victimized by them. To help them release their feelings ask them to talk to you about how they are feeling and why they have responded aggressively. You could also ask them to write down words or sentences, or illustrate their thoughts and feelings about this matter. If you are upset with each other, once you have both calmed down, discuss in more detail what has happened and why it has happened, learn about each other's perspective and agree on how your future interactions will be more respectful.

If children only make you aware of a one-off instance of maltreatment which they report to you when you are teaching, for example, name-calling, you may feel you do not have sufficient resources to give your full attention to their concerns. To help with these matters, teach children how to report bullying to a member of staff appropriately, for example, by asking to speak to their teacher after class, to thoroughly explain what has happened and how the bullying makes them feel, and be involved in making decisions of how their bullying will be dealt with. This might sound obvious but many children have not learnt how to complain effectively and this is rarely taught formally in school, although perhaps it should be!

When bullying is reported, investigate what happened before the event rather than just the incident reported. Consider how you can be more alert to bullying; can you observe and/or supervise children's interactions more? Often bullying is likely to occur where there is less supervision from staff such as in the playground, toilets and on the bus. You could work on a project with teachers over a half-term where you focus on observing and analyzing children's interactions more and finding out where bullying is present. Use this to improve how your school deals with children's specific issues of bullying.

Children are likely to thrive in a climate which supports and encourages them to improve. However, the process of change is difficult; it takes time and individuals may relapse. Provide children with opportunities and encouragement to improve their behaviour, and ensure those who are making progress receive recognition for their effort.

Support to 'Empower Practitioners'

Internal support to 'empower practitioners'

To deal effectively with bullying, develop your network of colleagues so you can effectively support pupils who are bullied, and improve your authority to handle conflict with pupils. Although teachers are legally obliged to tackle bullying you should not feel alone and unsupported in your attempts to resolve bullying. Speak with colleagues about the issues you are dealing with and pool together your thoughts and ideas so you can deal with it in the most effective ways. The 'empowering practitioners' approach is particularly applicable for areas of bullying that are complex and where there are 'grey' areas, so you can work with colleagues to investigate in depth the extent to which children are bullied and share good practice about how to approach the problem.

For school managers to 'empower practitioners' there ought to be systems in place which help staff feel confident about expressing their concerns around bullying, for example, through the staff ABAG where staff regularly meet to discuss bullying and how to manage it. Work with colleagues, school managers and pupils to develop strategies to develop more respectful ways for staff and pupils to interact and communicate with one another. Good classroom management can help you deal more effectively with bullying. Using firm but fair methods to control your class can help prevent children trying to take control of your class. It can also help to protect you from targeting certain children to establish control.

Bullying complaints involving school practitioners

If you feel bullied by a pupil you could speak to them on a one-to-one basis and explain that their behaviour is hurtful and unacceptable. If you feel particularly intimidated by them you might want to ask a colleague to attend the meeting with the pupil to support you. This could be a teacher who you think will deal with the issue effectively and/or a more senior member of staff. If you don't feel comfortable speaking with the pupil you could ask a senior member of staff to speak with the pupil on your behalf. If the bullying continues it will be necessary to inform your manager and the child's parents and complain about this behaviour more formally. It would be good practice for you to be involved in discussions with management about how the bullying will be handled to achieve the most effective outcomes. The 'healthy relationships' strategy will help you to develop a more positive relationship with pupils which can help resolve some conflict.

If you feel you are being bullied, or are perceived as bullying, it is important to draw upon your support network; for example, you could confide in a colleague who you trust. You may, at some stage, be accused of bullying another pupil. It can be difficult when accused of bullying because it is a stigmatizing term. However, look beyond the label to consider what behaviours you have engaged in which may have caused the pupil distress. There can be a fine line between reprimanding someone and making them feel targeted, or informing them that they need to improve their work and making them feel victimized. Clarify what the problem is that the pupil is finding problematic so you know exactly what the issue is; this gives you the opportunity to adjust your behaviour if necessary. Training on topics such as how to respond to conflict assertively might be helpful. Show your willingness to reflect on your behaviour, improve it and reach an agreement with the pupil and colleagues of how you will respectfully interact with pupils in future.

Although this book has not specifically researched workplace bullying, some approaches have been generated from my research findings about school bullying, and my consultancy/advisory roles in the workplace. If you feel bullied by colleagues keep a diary to record incidents, if there were any witnesses and how it makes you feel. If you feel able to do so, and you think it may be helpful, speak to the person bullying you, tell them their behaviour is upsetting you and ask them to stop. You could ask your organization if they can provide mediation for you both to prevent the problems escalating further. The TUC have found in their survey that 76 per cent of workers who reported incidents of bullying to their employer said that nothing had changed, or the situation got worse afterwards (Mackridge 2018) so seek informal resolution before you make a formal complaint. Some of the strategies in this book can be used to help resolve bullying between colleagues such as the victimized individual being involved in decisions about how their bullying is resolved and 'Mentoring for "Bullies"'. If you find the problems particularly stressful it can be beneficial to see if your organization provides counselling to support you to understand your feelings, release any anger you might have, and respond respectfully and appropriately. Find out if you can attend training on how to understand and manage bullying and improve how you respond to it.

If the bullying continues, consider making a complaint which can start informally and if not resolved could progress into a formal complaint. An informal complaint can be used as an initial phase of the formal complaints procedure. Being a member of a trade union can help you if you feel bullied by colleagues, parents or pupils, and if you are accused of bullying. Trade unions can support you to make formal complaints and represent you at formal meetings such as grievances. Ideally, after your complaint has been investigated there should be a meeting to discuss the most effective ways to prevent the bullying and help you move forward after the complaint.

Some school practitioners have informed me that they have felt bullied and intimidated by parents of pupils. This has been through parents being aggressive to them or complaining to the head about problems in their classroom before speaking to them first. If you feel bullied by parents then speak to colleagues and your manager and ask them to support you. You could speak to the parents concerned or ask your manager to explain to them that they are required to be respectful to staff. It can be helpful to have a policy on how parents and staff interact with each other respectfully. In your anti-bullying policy, you could incorporate bullying between colleagues, and bullying of school practitioners by parents into the document and specify how it should be addressed.

At some stage of your career you may be perceived as bullying colleagues. If you feel comfortable and you consider it is appropriate, speak to the person who feels bullied by you, ask them what aspect of your behaviour is causing them distress, discuss and consider whether it is reasonable for you to change your behaviour. If there is something about the accuser's behaviour that causes you distress, you could politely explain what this is, and if it is reasonable, ask them to adjust their behaviour. You could have development meetings with them to discuss the conflict and agree on how you will both interact more respectfully with one another in future. This discussion could be facilitated by a more senior member of staff and become more formal through having human resources (HR) and/or your trade union representatives involved. If a formal complaint is lodged against you, make sure you have read your organization's grievance and anti-bullying policy and seek advice from HR and your trade union representative about the process and what your rights are.

Policies and procedures: bullying involving school practitioners

It is important that you understand your employer's anti-bullying and grievance policy because if they do not follow their procedures you can appeal against the outcomes of their investigation. Your anti-bullying policies should be updated regularly and include a date when they will be reviewed. You could ask those who are updating your school's anti-bullying policy if you can have an input into how they are updated.

A policy about bullying between pupils and school staff should include the following: examples of what bullying between pupils and staff consist of; how bullying between pupils and staff can be reported; symptoms of bullying between pupils and staff; and strategies to resolve it, including an informal and formal way of reporting the bullying. To establish the anti-bullying policy between pupils and staff work with colleagues and pupils to find out what bullying between staff and pupils consists of, such as what examples they have experienced of this behaviour, and how it should be managed. Examples of teachers bullying pupils might include: rewarding all children in class apart from one child, humiliating remarks and shouting aggressively at children. Examples of pupils bullying teachers include: insulting remarks about their personal appearance, physical assault and swearing at them.

After you have discussed with pupils and colleagues the difference between teachers bullying their pupils and effective classroom management you can include this distinction in your anti-bullying policy. Of course, there will be some ambiguities and you might want to include some examples of these 'grey' areas. However, using examples which illustrate the difference between effective classroom management and teachers bullying their pupils can provide clarity on the matter. In essence, good classroom management should help children feel safe and that they are treated equally whereas bullying makes children feel targeted and distressed.

To support parents to report bullying, as recommended by the Department for Education (2017), write to parents/guardians informing them of your school's policies and providing website links of these policies so they can readily access them. To provide additional support you could facilitate training for parents/guardians to help them learn about how children can be bullied at school, how it should be dealt with and what they can do about it. You could also provide a forum for parents to meet regularly and discuss the well-being and behaviour of children and incorporate bullying in these discussions. A 'healthy relationships' policy can be included within your school's anti-bullying policy including details and examples of what these consist of, how they can be maintained and developed, and what to do when they are breached. To create this policy, speak with colleagues and pupils about what it should consist of. 'Healthy relationships' is a proactive approach which aims to bring about positive changes rather than just trying to stop bad behaviour. It could include how pupils and staff should speak to each other when they disagree with one another, and how teachers can respectfully explain to pupils that their behaviour is unacceptable. Elicit regular constructive feedback from children and colleagues about this multi-faceted anti-bullying policy so it can continue to be developed and updated.

External support to empower school practitioners

Find out if there are any external networks dealing with school bullying and associated problems with regular meetings in which you can participate. You can share and develop approaches to addressing bullying with colleagues in this network. Collaborate with external professionals who specialize in dealing with specific cases of bullying which you are finding particularly difficult to manage. There are charities such as Peacemakers who support schools in implementing restorative approaches to deal with bullying and interact more respectfully. Kidscape provide training to support children who are victimized by teaching them how to be more assertive, exercise their voice and build their confidence. Although these organizations are not necessarily pupil-led and tend not to specialize in dealing with the more nuanced cases of bullying, they can support children to improve how they respond to bullying. Drawing upon external professionals can provide educators with an additional layer of support, resources and expertise to combat bullying effectively.

Conclusion

This chapter has outlined your legal duty to tackle bullying, highlighted children's perspectives on how teachers handle bullying and has provided recommendations for good practice. The complex positioning of school practitioners has been discussed; for example, they are expected to deal with bullying in ways which most children do not consider to be effective. Children feel current methods for dealing with bullying often result in them being bullied even more for 'grassing'. Bullying is often taught in abstract ways, for example, through plays about fictional characters which tend to overlook children's lived experiences. Children feel that bulling would reduce if teachers listened more to pupils.

How pupils can be bullied by teachers, and how staff can bully each other, has been discussed. This chapter has provided guidance to empower practitioners to resolve bullying. The 'healthy relationships' approach can encourage pupils and staff to develop respectful interactions with one another and this can be incorporated into an anti-bullying policy. There should also be an anti-bullying policy which includes guidance on how to manage bullying between pupils and teachers.

The 'empathetic understanding' model has been discussed. This includes how staff can support pupils to enhance their understanding of their perspective, learn about the underlying issues behind problematic behaviour and agree how the problem will be resolved through development meetings. 'Empowering practitioners' outlines how you can draw upon external and internal support to strengthen your position in tackling bullying and how you can respond to complaints about bullying from various sources such as colleagues and pupils.

Chapter 4

Understanding and Resolving Systemic Bullying

Introduction

This chapter will enhance your understanding of the institutional and societal factors inherent in school which perpetuate bullying and outline how pupils and school practitioners can work together to combat these issues. Systemic bullying refers to how institutional and societal inequalities can position certain individuals, such as those with learning difficulties, as vulnerable, and contribute to them feeling victimized and distressed. How institutional factors can unfairly target children who are positioned as 'vulnerable', restrict their voice and encourage bullying is examined in this chapter. In addition, the adverse effects that inequality in school has on all children is examined.

Recommendations are provided to help you challenge the issues of systemic bullying. These include how the voice of pupils can be enhanced to reduce bullying and overt forms of punishment through 'empathetic understanding'. How 'Mentoring for "Bullies"' can support individuals who are involved in a vicious cycle of bullying to learn how to respond more respectfully to conflict is explained, including details of how you can implement this approach. 'Take responsibility' is discussed as a method for pupils and practitioners to exercise their agency and challenge systemic bullying.

The positioning of certain groups as vulnerable is often beyond the control of individual pupils and teachers in school. Ryan and Morgan (2011) argue that bullying is a manifestation of hierarchical operations of power in institutions. In schools, individuals are ranked based on their intellectual ability and placed into streams (such as the top, middle and lowest stream). Schools and society place high value on intellectual ability which, in effect, can contribute to the discrimination of individuals with learning difficulties. Arguably, teachers are expected to reinforce systems in school which inadvertently marginalize these children. They are required as part of their role to monitor the behaviour and performance of children, particularly those who are not performing at the standards expected of them. Teachers who work in schools which stream children are obliged to implement the ranking of children based on their perceived intellectual ability. However, to some extent, pupils and school practitioners can reinforce or challenge systemic bullying. They can also exercise agency in how they respond to individual children who feel marginalized and help them feel included.

Furthermore, children can feel coerced into reinforcing hierarchies in school where those positioned as 'vulnerable' are subject to bullying rather than challenge these hierarchies (Nassem 2017). Systemic bullying is currently an under-researched area as most research still focuses on bullying between individual pupils. The traditional approach focuses primarily on dealing with aggressive behaviour of a minority of pathologized individuals and does not address the systemic factors which contribute to bullying or provide meaningful strategies to challenge the underlying cause. The whole-school approach developed by the traditional perspective of bullying aims to involve all members of the school community in tackling bullying. However, the social-ecological model provides a more dynamic lens to address bullying than the traditional and whole-school approach by taking into account bullying at multiple levels: individual, peers, school and communities (Swearer and Hymel 2015). Although the social-ecological model provides a more contextualized understanding than the traditional and whole-school approach, it does not sufficiently address the systemic issues which contribute to bullying. The whole-school approach and social-ecological perspective do not consider the fluidity of power struggles or pay sufficient attention to the complexity of the positioning and role of staff in handling and, in some cases, being subject to bullying. These approaches do not consider the complex ways power operates (and can be abused) through institutional structures which instil societal inequalities from the child's perspective, or take ambiguities into consideration. However, the empirical research which underpins this book will help you draw upon children's perceptions to understand the nuanced ways children experience systemic bullying.

Researchers who consider systemic bullying, such as Walton (for example, 2005, 2010) tend to adopt a theoretical rather than empirical lens which does not sufficiently consider how bullying is experienced from the child's point of view. Although Bansel *et al.* (2009) use a theoretical approach to examine children's views, it is through the retrospective experience of researchers rather than focusing on the child's current perspective. There are currently few recommendations of how to tackle systemic bullying by drawing upon the child's voice. However, this chapter will help you understand children's experiences of systemic bullying so you can work with pupils and staff to challenge the problem.

Systemic Bullying: The Evidence

Intellectual ability

'Thick' label

Most children with learning difficulties, in the lower streams and the PRU felt they were perceived as 'thick' and internalized this label by believing that being in a low stream represented a substantial part of their ability and identity. Several children in the lower streams reported 'I feel thick' and 'I'm thick'. Kimberly reported that 'we're bottom because we're thickest' (Year 7, Highcross Private School). The hierarchies and ranks children were placed in created an abnormal shameful class of pupils who were placed under surveillance.

Some teachers referred to children in the lowest streams in derogatory and humiliating ways. A teacher at Highcross Private School explained how they referred to children in the lowest stream: 'We call them the diddlydonks' and another teacher explained: 'They're not the brightest.' The PRU was perceived in a stigmatized way as being for children who are not intelligent. It was commonly referred to by the pupils who attended as a 'window licker' or 'spaca school'. Children felt that attending a PRU meant they were marginalized from society, stigmatized and perceived as unintelligent. As Vanessa explains, 'Nobody sees anybody here as clever, all students are like, "you're here for same reasons, we're all retards"' (Year 10, Priory Lane PRU).

However, some children who felt they were perceived as 'thick' because they were in the lowest streams also felt they were more capable than other people realized. Although Kimberly stated earlier that she was in the bottom stream because she was the 'thickest', she also said, 'They think that you're thick but you're actually not' (Year 7, Highcross Private School). This finding was more prevalent in the private school, where children had to pass a test to attend. However, it demonstrates how children can exercise some agency over how they are classified and labelled and how children's perception of their intellectual ability can change.

Streaming

Streaming was constructed as a cause of much conflict and bullying. Being in a 'bottom' stream can contribute to distress, anger and self-loathing; it is a place where no one wants to be. Children who did not conform to academic standards expected of them felt isolated and rejected which can be perceived as bullying. As this book suggests, and as Epp and Watkinson (1997) explain, the hierarchies and measures that streaming places on children and how they are excluded from certain groups is systemic bullying when children are distressed or burdened by this. Some children considered upsetting someone because of their disability to be bullying. When asked the question 'What is bullying?' a pupil replied: 'It's making somebody upset by their disability.' This highlights how important an individual's feelings are and that bullying is associated with issues of inequality in society where people can be bullied just because they belong to a devalued group. School practitioners and children can reinforce this inequality and victimize these children. When I interviewed Helen, she was profoundly distressed by being bullied because of her learning difficulties:

> I came to high school not knowing how to read or write and I used to get bullied for that, well, I still get bullied. I can't read books or I can't copy down writing or do long writing because I just start crying because my brain's not active enough (starts to cry)… It just makes me feel dumb.
>
> (Helen, Year 10, Townville School)

Helen demonstrates how children can lose control over their emotions when they are bullied because of their learning difficulties. A boy made her angry when he said she 'couldn't read'. She responded aggressively when she 'got him up to [the] wall'. Being classified as unintelligent is not something children can escape from by changing schools. The construction of learning difficulties places these children under surveillance, and stigmatizes and marginalizes them throughout their lives.

In the lower streams, children's achievements were often not appreciated by pupils. Despite their best efforts they usually could not escape the stigma that their low positioning subjects them to. Often children with learning difficulties were bullied persistently by different people. Martin (who was in the highest stream at Woodlands School) explains, 'Normally it'd be brainy groups that they'd pick for best work but people that have needs and stuff they tend to pick them because they're not right good.' Martin feels the children in the lower streams are inferior, is resentful towards them when they are rewarded and believes that they do not have skills worthy of recognition. Laura refers to being in the lowest stream as a form of discipline and sanction:

> Laura: I want good grades, I don't want to be really brainy but I don't want to be really dumb, I want to be in the middle.
> Interviewer: How would you feel if you were in stream B2?
> Laura: I'd feel mad with myself that I tried my best but I got a punishment.
>
> (Laura, Year 7, Highcross Private School)

Laura implies that being in the lowest stream would cause her personal suffering and anger, and that she would feel offended and victimized as a consequence. Because of the negative consequences of being in the 'top' or 'bottom' stream, which could subject children on either extreme to bullying, several pupils suggested that being in the middle stream was better. The creation of a 'good' and 'bad' group was a way of normalizing people, as suggested by Foucault (1979) and was inherent in bullying. Being in the middle stream created less visibility. However, children who were in the highest streams were not as stigmatized as those in the lowest streams.

Children in the lower streams or who had learning difficulties spoke more frequently about being unfairly punished, put in isolation, sent out of class, and asked to do work which was beyond their ability, which often made them feel humiliated and distressed. This is considered as systemic bullying. When the teacher is involved and upsets children because of this, it is considered as bullying by teachers. Stephanie is dyslexic and explains how she felt too embarrassed to read in class and was punished by her teacher as a consequence:

> I said, 'Miss, I'm not being funny but I'm not reading out loud because I'm not very good at reading', she went, 'So what, just read out loud' and I said, 'No' so she gave me a detention.
>
> (Stephanie, Year 10, Parklane School)

Even material in school, such as displays on the wall, reinforced the inferiority of children who had difficulties with reading, for example I observed a postcard on the wall of a classroom which read, 'boys who read are superior beings'; this demonstrates how children can feel systemically bullied solely through observation.

Children in the top streams and several children in private school explained how they felt they were not always able to reach the standards expected of them and often felt inferior to other children who they were compared to: 'You're expected to set a standard but, in some subjects, you can't step to that standard because you're not as good in them as another person' (Tamara, Year 7, Highcross Private School). This created a sense of 'never being good enough'.

Just because pupils can be bullied for being at either extreme of the intellectual ability spectrum does not mean that they are on a par with each other. 'An education' and getting a good job were perceived as important elements of school. Children perceived getting 'an education' as getting high-grade GCSEs (A to Cs). Helen explains, 'In the end it's all about education because you need GCSEs to get a good job, good GCSEs' (Helen, Year 10, Townville School).

Although most children reported that 'school is OK', children with learning difficulties or who were badly behaved often stated that they did not like school. This could be because they are less likely to gain the 'good education' that was considered to be important. Jack referred to school as 'a load of rubbish' (Year 8, Parklane School, second interview). He felt that 'swots' were treated better than him and were the 'teacher's pet'. Pupils who were bullied for being a 'swot' were not usually subject to as much punishment from teachers or picked out unfavourably by them; they also have a greater chance of achieving good qualifications. Jack felt there were long-term advantages to being a 'swot' as 'when you grow up you get a good education'. He implies that he is not having a good education because he is not succeeding academically.

Social Class and Punishments
Punishments and marginalization

As previously mentioned, children from working-class backgrounds who had learning difficulties often felt targeted by their peers, teachers and the school system. These children were from particularly economically deprived working-class backgrounds and their parents were usually unemployed or earned low salaries. They often preferred to conform to their peer group and be connected to their local community rather than obey their teachers and achieve academic success. Most of these children were males but there some females from this socio-economic background who also experienced this cycle of victimization. They could receive the same punishment for a wide range of behaviours, such as being sent out of class for forgetting a pencil or being aggressive to a teacher/pupil. This is a zero-tolerance policy and can be associated with Foucault's (1979) suggestion that the best way to avoid serious offences is to punish the minor seriously. However, being punished and marginalized usually did not improve children's behaviour and resulted in further punishment, resentment and feelings of victimization.

PRUs can be perceived as putting all the 'bad kids' together, making their behaviour worse and segregating them from mainstream society. 'They've had bad experiences in their lives and you get used to listening to 'em talking about being naughty and then you be naughty and you can't help it' (Duncan, Year 11, Priory Lane PRU). Although these marginalized pupils were persistently reprimanded by their teachers and frequently felt 'picked on' they generally did not directly refer to this as bullying. Tristan subjected his Maths teacher, Steve, to personal insults about his personal appearance by frequently referring to him as 'Egghead'. When I interviewed Tristan, he explained how he felt targeted by Steve. 'Steve, I've tried to crack him so many times…because every time someone said something, he always said "Tristan", even when it wasn't me he still said "Tristan". Like, fucking "don't be saying me you gimp"' (Tristan, Year 11, Priory Lane PRU).

Boredom, as discussed in Chapter 2, was a common experience in school and although some children tried to overcome boredom many felt they could not. Arguably, children could concentrate on their work in lessons to occupy themselves and deter boredom. This was not a choice every child could equally make. Oliver's learning difficulties were so significant that it was extremely difficult to for him to concentrate in his lessons:

Interviewer: What do you think people expect of you?

Oliver: To work.

Interviewer: And why won't you do it?

Oliver: I just can't do it. I get told answers and half way through writing it I forget it and that's what annoys me so I don't do my work. I give up too easy.

Interviewer: What makes you give up?

Oliver: Forgetting that answer and then getting wound up and just not doing it at all.

Interviewer: Why do you think teachers are expected to control their class?

Oliver: They're in charge of the lesson, aren't they?

Interviewer: Why can't pupils control themselves?

Oliver: Work that you get given.

(Oliver, Year 10, Priory Lane PRU)

In my opinion, boredom was particularly problematic for children who were the most disengaged from school, for example, with learning difficulties and/or who usually misbehaved or were in the PRUs. Newberry and Duncan (2001) also found that children who engaged in a high level of delinquent behaviours had a higher tendency to experience boredom. In the quotation below, Grant explains how when he is placed in isolation he sits, facing a board, for several days and with nothing to do. He suggests that being placed in isolation can cause harmful psychological and physiological side-effects:

> Can't do isolation me, never done it, never can, I've always walked out of it, I can't just sit there and look at a blackboard cos you have boards, don't you, like boards going up, you always sit there...you don't do shit, sit there for six hours, what's point. I get migraines me; big migraines.
>
> (Grant, Year 11, Priory Lane PRU)

Children who are punished through the school's disciplinary system, for example being given detention or put in isolation, felt it increased their boredom which made them feel frustrated and angry. Their boredom was associated with a sense of emptiness, entrapment and detachment which stripped away their morality and made them feel unfairly victimized.

Pupil Voice
Restricted voice
When people are bullied their sense of agency and voice becomes increasingly restricted. The problem ranges from children who argue with their teacher and who lose their voice when they are punished, to those who are obedient, suppress their voice and do not question their teachers.

Martin implies that teachers don't always respond effectively to the views of children and that, as a consequence, children may not know how to exercise their voice effectively:

> Martin: It'd be better in lessons and all, if you wanna say something about lesson and can put your hand up and say what your point of view is and how you'll work it out.
> Interviewer: Do we listen to one another's point of view respectfully?

Martin: Not really, when she [teacher] says, 'Let's start writing and do it' and then someone puts their hand up they'll [the teacher] say, 'I'll be back here in a minute' and when they do, you don't express yourself right as much as you want to.

(Martin, Year 7, Woodlands School)

Working-class 'voice'

Walton (2005) asserts that research has yet to fully address how bullying is characterized by negative associations with difference, such as social class which this chapter addresses. To date, current research has yet to adequately address these issues. Working-class males are often pressured to respond aggressively by their peers, and they are rewarded for doing so (Willis 1977; Mac an Ghaill 1994). Consequently, they are punished and placed under the attention of professionals, thereby creating an environment of tensions and conflict from which bullying stems (Walton 2010).

Children who overtly resisted their teachers' authority in the state school tended to be working-class boys who sometimes spoke to their teachers aggressively and felt 'picked on' and unfairly punished by them. Once identified by teachers for being disobedient, they were subject to increasing surveillance, normalization (pressures to obey their teachers) and punishment. This vicious cycle is considered as a form of systemic bullying by teachers when teachers reinforce the cycle which causes children to feel hurt as a consequence. It can be associated with Foucault's notion that certain groups are used to establish the power of the dominant class (Foucault 1979, 1980). Children who feel marginalized and targeted can take their anger out on you which can contribute to the formation of hostile and tense relationships.

Through misbehaving, children resisted their teacher's authority, but they also became increasingly subject to being supervised and punished by them. Arguably, these children would have more power if they resisted being under surveillance and punished by teachers through behaving obediently. Often, children who overtly resisted their teacher's authority did not express their views formally or respectfully to their teachers and tended to be rude and insulting towards them, as demonstrated in the previous chapter. However, these children may not have known how to effectively articulate their voice.

At times, the learning difficulties some of these children had made it difficult for them to exercise their voice. One child, Gavin, was asked to write down information for a psychologist about 'what a teacher should know about pupils'. However, his severe dyslexia meant he could not articulate his views adequately through writing.

Children reported that although teachers may not have much power in resolving bullying, they hold ultimate power over them when they try to exercise their voice by disagreeing with teachers. In the PRU, Simon (Year 10) explains, 'No one listens anyway in this school.' He believed that pupils' views are ignored and not taken seriously. Simon also felt that people who knew his views would think of him: 'What a cunt.' He feels he is seen as shameful and his views are dismissed.

Many children felt it was unfair that they were not treated with consideration by teachers but were expected to obey their teachers. Children who were the most vocal about this issue were predominantly working-class boys in the state school and PRU. Grant (Year 11, Priory Lane PRU) asserts that, 'Just because I'm a pupil that doesn't mean that I have to be treated with less respect, that I should have to give them respect but they're giving me no respect.'

Several children, particularly those who were working-class with learning difficulties, often spoke candidly and unashamedly about being bullied by personal comments about their physical appearance such as 'people call me sumo' and 'they used to call me malteser head and that cos of like shape of my head [points to head].' Although many of these children did not report bullying to their teachers, they resisted the isolation of being silent about their abuse and talked openly about their experiences, as noted by Zerubabel (2006). Alex said he couldn't be happier in his personal circumstances and home life such as having a horse in his back garden and living with his grandma. However, children tormented him about this and referred to him as a 'gypo'. Even though other children tried to belittle Alex and treat him as inferior, he maintained a sense of worth and appreciation for his lifestyle which he was bullied for. This highlights how individuals can resist the negative perceptions of others by perceiving themselves positively. However, the persistent bullying and derogatory way children from deprived backgrounds with learning difficulties were treated may eventually make them feel ashamed of themselves and their circumstances which is likely to weaken their psychological resistance to being bullied.

'Good pupil' voice

Children who were very obedient and succeeding academically, particularly in the private school, also had their voice restricted and usually respected the power of their teachers. Jessica (Year 7, Highcross

Private School) explains, 'They've already been at school and learnt everything so we accept that.' They were often more restrained in expressing their feelings and felt pressured to conform to school rules and norms. Laura describes what she has learnt from being on the school council: 'You get to know what people want and what you can't have' (Year 7, Highcross Private School). Through being on the school council Laura is learning about how children are limited rather than how she can help make positive changes for the pupils she represents. Consequently, these children had submitted part of their autonomy and voice. However, through not overtly challenging school systems or their teacher's authority, there can be long-term benefits such as improved opportunities to succeed in their education (Bourdieu 1990). Several children in the private school did not exercise their voice in such a strong or emotional way as children from the other schools. They were not as expressive about their emotions and experiences and were more compliant than the other children. This was particularly pronounced for children in the higher streams where they were highly obedient, and seemed to be working hard to ensure their school was presented positively. Impett *et al.* (2008) argue that middle-class girls are pressured to be the 'perfect girl' and censor their thoughts, emotions and behaviours to maintain relationships, resulting in a discrepancy between what they think, feel and say, which is associated with low self-esteem. It could be argued that being highly obedient can result in children's inner moral guidance being filtered out if they allow other people to direct their behaviours and pass responsibility for its consequences on to others (Milgram 1963).

In the private school, girls had to wear skirts, and in the state schools, girls had to wear a skirt for netball matches regardless of how cold the weather was. Their bodies were objects of control and manipulation, as suggested by Foucault (1979). Girls in the private school justified this ruling in terms of it enhancing their femininity by making them 'look like a girl'. The private school discourages girls from having control over their bodies and when they resisted this power they were punished. 'It was a really freezing cold netball match and I had my trackie bottoms on and Miss gave me a red card' (Kimberly, Year 7, Highcross Private School). Sandra (Year 7) explained that although there had been several petitions for girls to wear trousers in the private school the headteacher persistently crushed their resistance and the status quo remained. Like most of the other girls, Sandra accepted the headteacher's ruling: 'I'd like trousers but I'm fine with skirts, we've tried to campaign for trousers but the headmaster says no.'

Being 'feminine' was not as important to girls in the state schools and a minority of girls suggested that girls who wear skirts may also be perceived in a more sexual way. Stephanie explained that she always wears trousers, so that a male teacher who 'looks up girls' skirts' cannot look up hers. In this respect, she resisted her teacher having power over her body and protected herself by controlling his gaze:

> We're allowed to wear skirts for school, and he'll walk past and drop a pencil so he can bend down and look under the table, and if you're walking out of classroom, he'll look at your bum; that's why I always wear trousers.
>
> (Stephanie, Year 10, Parklane School)

Several children, particularly well-behaved and middle-class girls, subtly resisted authority and exercised some control. They were less likely to be identified as boys who were frequently identified by their teachers as misbehaving. Whilst these 'bad boys' were placed under surveillance, obedient children often escaped being supervised and punished by teachers:

> Sarah: You're not allowed to wear black trainers, but I've got some, but I never get caught...they don't really look at mine.
> Interviewer: Whose trainers do they look at?
> Sarah: Like all bad people.
>
> (Sarah, Year 11, Townville School)

Sarah demonstrates that ways of disciplining children can be unfair and allow those who tend to be obedient and conforming to escape being targeted and punished. Subsequently their infractions of the school rules are usually concealed.

Agency

Often children suggested their agency was strongly bounded by inequalities in school and society which influenced their personal circumstances. Several children permanently excluded from school discussed having restricted choices; most of these were a consequence of their exclusion. They were able to gain few qualifications, regardless of how hard they worked and often suggested that they are 'gonna get nothing out of it [i.e. school]'.

Several children excluded from school or who were often punished suffered from family problems, which restricted their chances of succeeding highly in education, Melanie, aged 15, who was in the PRU, informed me that she lives alone 'in a caravan because I got moved about'. Being excluded from school and coming from a disadvantaged background were strongly associated with one another (as found by De Pear and Garner 1996). This research supports the widely held finding that children from deprived backgrounds have less chance of succeeding in education, which limits their agency (Hodkinson and Bloomer 2001). If children had great difficulties in reading it made it extremely difficult, and in some cases impossible, for them to do their work. Jack discussed wanting to enter the army 'because there's hardly no writing'. However, there is some fluidity, as agency was exercised by children throughout their school day, for example, some children who frequently misbehaved attempted to improve their behaviour. Shaun (Year 8, Townville School) was excluded from class for forgetting his pencil, but explains, 'My mum's bought me 50 pencils from the pound shop and 20 pens so I can't forget 'em now.'

After being repeatedly punished, a few children became obedient and compliant. They stopped resisting the teacher's authority and suppressed their voice. Jack explained that when he is placed in isolation he feels like 'going back out there and telling 'em what I feel like'. However, he explained that he now suppresses his thoughts and feelings and no longer shares them with his teachers. He has learned that, although he is treated unfairly, 'they're always gonna beat you'. Jack has become more compliant because he feels overpowered. He has learned to accept the restrictions on his power and his low positioning.

Excluded pupils who will not achieve any qualifications, and who struggle to do their work, can give up because there is such a low likelihood of success. There were children in the PRU who believed that if they remained in the PRU their life would be ruined. 'All people that are bosses of all schools they just threw us in a corner and said, "They can be dossers of the world"' (Seth, Year 10, Priory Lane PRU). This can be linked with Foucault's (1979) writings on the restricted agency of delinquents where once identified as a delinquent it was difficult for them to be anything else. Oliver feels that it is too difficult to improve his circumstances and he doesn't try to improve anymore:

Interviewer: Do you think deep down that you could do well at something?
Oliver: If I tried.
Interviewer: And do you think you're ever gonna try?

Oliver: No.
Interviewer: Why not?
Oliver: Too hard.

(Oliver, Year 10, Priory Lane PRU)

Oliver wanted to leave the PRU by going to college but he was aware that he was unlikely to get the opportunity and saw little point in trying to study. Audrey (who organized placements for the pupils in the PRU) informed me that there was 'no chance' that Oliver would be offered a place at college as staff felt his academic ability was too low and that they would be ridiculed and 'laughed at' if they recommended him.

On the other hand, children who were obedient and studious usually could gain practical benefits from the school system and so had an interest in conforming to it (Bourdieu 1990). They often had the abilities and opportunities to succeed academically and tended to be in the high streams and/or in private school:

I always try and do my best, try and get better, sometimes it's hard because if last time you did an absolutely great one it's hard to keep up to the same standard but as long as you keep on trying.

(Paul, Year 7, Highcross Private School)

Although children in the private school tended to have financial and familial support to succeed in education, the girls had their agency restricted to the extent that they weren't even allowed to wear trousers. Catherine tried to succeed even though she had been permanently excluded from school and placed in a PRU. She explained that 'my grandma would pay for me to go to university'. Children who had been marginalized but who were striving to improve their circumstances did not want to follow the traditional biography expected of them and exercised their agency by improving their lives: 'I wanna prove them wrong that I can actually do something.' To succeed, children who had misbehaved were beginning to be obedient and studious and accept their teachers' authority (even though they didn't always agree with it). These pupils resisted their expected life path and strove for more educational opportunities. In giving up their resistance, they gained greater power by improving their opportunities to 'get a good job' and reduced their punishments from teachers.

How to Address Systemic Bullying

Although there is little research on how to combat systemic bullying, the recommendations in this chapter will help you make a good start, and collaborate with colleagues and pupils to make a positive difference.

Improve your understanding of systemic bullying

Remember to look beyond the 'bully' and 'victim' labels and consider bullying as a spectrum of aggressive (overt and/or covert) interactions that range from mild to severe. Consider how pupils and staff can be positioned to target those marginalized such as by placing children with learning difficulties in the lowest streams which can contribute to their distress and feelings of victimization. To enhance your understanding of systemic bullying, participate in training and development about the issue; this is discussed in the following chapter.

Collaborate with pupils, staff and parents to create a shared and robust definition of systemic bullying which is promoted widely across school and referred to regularly. Once you have developed a robust definition of systemic bullying for your school, explain to children, parents and colleagues what it consists of.

Use a holistic approach to combat systemic bullying
Consult with pupils and staff to resolve systemic bullying

To combat systemic bullying, liaise with a core team of pupils and colleagues to learn about the issues and develop strategies to overcome these. If you have a pupil and staff ABAG, ask them what features of the school system are causing problems for children and staff in relation to bullying, and what ought to be changed. Collaborate with the pupil and staff ABAG to develop an action plan showing which aspects of school should be improved to tackle systemic bullying and how. This knowledge should be presented to senior managers to improve understanding of systemic bullying and school practices to resolve it.

Involve families

Establish a forum for parents to meet regularly with staff such as teachers and those who work in pastoral care. In this forum, consult with parents to find out what support they require from the school to help prevent their children from being bullied, and to help you resolve bullying effectively. You might feel there are familial issues which are contributing to children's engagement in bullying. For example, you might think a child who is aggressive might have learnt this behaviour from their parents and/or siblings. Ask parents if there are any matters about school and/or home which they would like to talk about. Discuss with parents and colleagues how the school and parents can work together to overcome any problems which may have arisen between them.

'Mentoring for "Bullies"' to combat systemic bullying

The 'Mentoring for "Bullies"' programme can be used to help tackle systemic bullying. To overcome systemic issues affecting the mentee, speak with them about what aspects of school they can and cannot change and how they can improve their lives. This will help them understand their positioning within school. Mentoring can support children to succeed in a system which they often feel is against them. It enables children to effectively express their voice without being complacent, unfairly punished or marginalized. Through mentoring, children can make informed decisions about how they behave and construct their circumstances. Although mentoring is confidential and specific cases cannot be discussed with others, some generic recommendations may develop which can enhance school governance and how teachers support pupils.

'Healthy relationships' to overcome systemic bullying

Encourage children to accept themselves and not be ashamed of who they are. Several children in this chapter were adversely influenced by how other children and teachers perceived them. When pupils felt they were perceived as 'thick' they often felt inferior and distressed as a consequence. Remember to teach children how to internally challenge the negative things people say about them which have caused distress and instead construct themselves more positively. Support children to be less reliant on the opinions other people have of them and improve how they perceive themselves.

'Take responsibility' to improve pupils' behaviour

At the beginning of the academic year, encourage children to make a new start. Explain how they can improve their behaviour and academic performance. Help children develop responses to challenge their negative thoughts which restrict them from trying to reach their potential. Teach children how to exercise their autonomy and how they can make decisions which improve their personal circumstances. Remind children of how they can exercise their autonomy throughout the academic year. Encourage children to exercise their agency through conducting independent research and writing reports of their findings on a topic they select from a range of specified topics. Because children can exercise some control in what they learn they are likely to feel more stimulated which is likely to decrease boredom and the associated side-effects.

Reflect with colleagues on what subjects are actually necessary for children to be streamed in. You could use streaming in the subjects only when you are preparing pupils for their GCSEs if they are taking the same subject but different level examinations such as in English, Science or Maths. A more fluid approach to differentiation may encourage children to improve their academic performance rather than feeling that there are few opportunities to succeed because they are in the lower streams. Furthermore, a less rigid approach to classifying children based on their intellectual ability could help prevent children in the lower streams from feeling 'thick' and distressed by this. It can also help reduce the bullying which might arise between children in the highest and lowest streams.

'Empathetic understanding'
A 'system of dialogue' to improve behaviour
There ought to be space in your school's discipline system for children to meet with an allocated member of staff and talk to them about their behaviour when they misbehave. Your disciplinary system should provide children with the opportunity to explain why they have behaved the way they have done and receive an appropriate response from a relevant member of staff.

In some schools, children who misbehave complete a form to write down what has happened, how they have made other people feel, why they shouldn't have done it, and how they are going to make things better. Children who have difficulties with writing can choose from a selection of emojis (for example, with sad and happy faces) and words such as 'I hurt someone' or 'I damaged something'. However, through a 'system of dialogue' children can speak with a member of staff so they can understand what they have done wrong and do not feel they are being unfairly punished. Having dialogue with children about why their behaviour is unacceptable is likely to reduce detentions, exclusions and repeated misbehaviour. Practise and rehearse with children how they can respond more respectfully to conflict. Agree a means of communicating regularly with children who misbehave with colleagues and school managers. This 'system of dialogue' could be incorporated into your behaviour management policy.

The school's behavioural management team can collaboratively review and update behavioural policies, and meet regularly to improve school processes for responding to children's negative behaviour. This team could also consist of class teachers, staff responsible for pastoral care, learning mentors and colleagues who want to get more involved in dealing with behavioural management at a strategic level. Once you have asked pupils who have misbehaved to explain their behaviour, share your perspective with them and share how other pupils and colleagues may feel about their behaviour. This will encourage them to reflect on their behaviour and understand the effects it is having on others.

A clear system for monitoring which children are being punished, and when, can alert staff to which children are being persistently punished. This could be made more accessible to staff online. Speak with these children to find out why they are not improving their behaviour and explore with these pupils what would help improve their behaviour. Find out if there are any underlying factors which are contributing to the problem. Involve the pupil's parents/guardians in these conversations so you can understand the broader issues involved and support children and families to make long-term improvements. From conversations with these pupils you might be able to make recommendations to improve your school's disciplinary strategy. After speaking with staff and pupils about your school's disciplinary system you might find that certain means of punishment are not as effective as they should be. Reflect with colleagues and pupils on how your current systems of punishment can be improved and if some are perceived to be ineffective discuss what they might be replaced with.

Consider the appropriateness and severity of the punishments you and your school subject children to. Although, in some cases it may be necessary to remove a child from class, for example when they are harming themselves or others. Instead of putting children in isolation for several days or suspending them from school you could arrange for children to go on retreat for a few days. Retreats could be provided in a building on school premises which specifically caters to supporting these students. You might be able to provide retreats away from school. They can provide intensive support by staff in order to improve the behaviour of children who are persistently in trouble for misbehaving. Retreats aim to provide an in-depth opportunity for pupils to have regular dialogue, reflection, mentoring and support from school practitioners to improve their behaviour. There could also be support to help children with their school work whilst they are on retreat to make sure that they progress with their learning.

Incorporate pupil voice into school systems

My research findings highlight that pupils feel their voice is suppressed and much more support is needed to encourage them to exercise their voice. Ensure your school council represents a diverse range of pupils from those who are obedient and succeeding highly to those who are disobedient and struggling with their work. Support children in the school council to learn how to effectively challenge other pupils, staff and school policy, and improve practices in school. Teach them how to respectfully articulate their views and improve their school ethos.

In the pupil and staff ABAG, address issues of bullying between pupils, pupils and teachers, and systemic bullying; and how to deal it. These should be discussed as ongoing items on the ABAG's agenda. It can provide children with opportunities to express their views about your school's disciplinary system and how it can be developed. Ask children what they think about your school's approach to dealing with unacceptable behaviour. Speak to pupils to find out how they think the way school punishes them can be improved in order to deter negative behaviour, and how your school can instil positive behaviour and a sense of justice where children feel they are treated fairly. The pupil ABAG can feed into the school council as well as the staff ABAG. If you do not want to establish an additional group to the school council you could incorporate the pupil ABAG into the school council by having issues of bullying, including systemic bullying, and how to combat it, as a standing item on the agenda.

Challenge discriminatory practices

Provide more awareness and support to protect children from being discriminated against by pupils and staff based on their social class, gender and/or for having learning difficulties/disabilities. Ask children to reflect on times when they have heard or engaged in disablist language and what this consists of. Emphasize how disablist language is unacceptable. Reflect with children on how they feel when they are called 'thick' and how you can work together to help people feel better if they are referred to in this way. Develop plans of action showing how colleagues and pupils can prevent individuals being discriminated against by staff and pupils because they may have a disability.

Encourage colleagues to reflect on how they might inadvertently cause distress to children because they have learning difficulties/ disabilities. Discuss with colleagues the language which is used to refer to children who are struggling academically and how staff and pupils interact with these children. Consider how children are rewarded in school for their achievements; if systems for rewarding children are fair; and how you can improve the way you motivate children and recognize their success. Keep your knowledge up to date about issues of disability through reading and participating in training on the issue. This will help protect you from inadvertently discriminating against pupils with disabilities. Consider what messages staff might be communicating about pupils with learning difficulties/disabilities through the hidden curriculum[1] and the information inadvertently taught to children, such as displays on the wall. Some pupils might conceal the extent of their learning difficulties so if you suspect they are doing so, then investigate the matter further and find out whether any additional support could be provided or increased.

Respectfully discuss with children and colleagues how issues of social class, gender and perceived intellectual ability can be associated with bullying. Talk about how hostilities and tensions might arise between children who appear to be given favourable treatment and those who feel marginalized. Consider how children might feel resentful to those who are perceived as receiving favourable treatment, and how children from particularly deprived communities can feel segregated in school. Ask children if, and how, their peers might be treated unfairly in school and what they think can be done to treat children more equally. The pupil ABAG could work with the staff ABAG to investigate and address issues of disablist bullying and bullying which involve issues of social class inequalities. Be aware of how children from deprived backgrounds, particularly males, can find it difficult to conform to educational norms (Willis 1977) and collaborate with their families to help them make informed choices about their behaviour, and improve how they perceive their education.

Reflect on what children are informally learning from school through the hidden curriculum about themselves and other individuals. The previous discussion in this chapter about how girls have to wear skirts

---

1   The hidden curriculum refers to the transmission of unofficial norms, values and beliefs inadvertently learned in the classroom and the social environment.

in the private school (and for PE in the state schools) indicates how girls' bodies can become the objects of control and manipulation through following rules which can be seen as sexist and make some girls feel vulnerable to sexual abuse. We need to ensure that the rules children are obliged to follow do not discriminate against certain groups.

Allowing children to decide whether or not to wear skirts can help them take control of their body and feel empowered. Furthermore, when pupils are petitioning about an issue it is worthwhile to meet with the group of pupils, or representatives who they allocate, to investigate what the issues are and how they can be resolved. To help protect staff and pupils from experiencing, or being perceived as engaging in, sexually inappropriate behaviour, colleagues should discuss and agree what behaviours between staff and pupils are sexually appropriate and inappropriate ways of interacting. Ensure you also talk about the 'grey' areas and nuances. Speak about how staff and pupils can respectfully challenge sexually inappropriate behaviour and how to encourage children to behave more respectfully. Approach the issue of what constitutes sexually appropriate and inappropriate behaviour amongst colleagues and how this might be addressed; this will help you provide a good example for pupils to follow.

Anti-bullying policy for tackling systemic bullying

The pupil and staff ABAGs can work together to develop an anti-bullying policy between pupils and staff which address issues of systemic bullying and provide strategies to resolve these issues. After consulting with staff and pupils about systemic bullying, include in your anti-bullying policy: what constitutes systemic bullying; the effects of systemic bullying on pupils and staff; and how it will be addressed. Include in your policy examples of the systemic issues which are associated with bullying such as how children with learning difficulties can feel repeatedly punished and marginalized, and include some of the strategies recommended in this chapter to combat these issues. Specify in your anti-bullying policies how you will review and develop systems for disciplining children. You could include the 'Mentoring for "Bullies"' programme in your anti-bullying policy as a system of support for children who persistently engage in bullying who feel marginalized and persistently punished to respond more respectfully to conflict.

Include in your anti-bullying policy that staff will collaborate with pupils, colleagues and parents to improve how bullying (including systemic bullying) is addressed. For staff to lead by example they ought to feel they are treated with respect by colleagues, managers and parents. It is difficult for staff to feel they can help children who are bullied if they feel bullied themselves. Senior managers should find out what support staff feel they need to effectively combat all forms of bullying including systemic bullying. The pupil and staff ABAG could help you improve your school's policy on systemic bullying. This could include guidance for staff about how they should respectfully communicate and respond to pupils who are struggling to do their work or who are persistently misbehaving. Furthermore, your anti-bullying policy should enable children to report bullying orally and not just in a written format as some children have difficulties articulating themselves through writing. Teach your anti-bullying policy to children including what constitutes bullying and how bullying is dealt with by school. Develop a child-friendly anti-bullying policy with children so they understand what to do about it. Ensure that all your anti-bullying policy/policies are written clearly so that they can be clearly read, understood and applied by children, parents and colleagues.

Conclusion

This chapter has discussed the complex problem of systemic bullying which you are likely to be confronted with in your school. It has explained how working-class males who have learning difficulties can particularly experience systemic bullying. However, there are widespread issues of inequality which influence all pupils and suppress their voice. How middle-class children, particularly girls, can have their voice suppressed and be pressured to be controlled and compliant has also been discussed. The ways in which systemic inequalities in school oppress children and contribute to bullying amongst pupils, and between pupils and staff, have been explored.

To combat systemic bullying, there has been guidance on how pupils, school practitioners and parents can have input into improving how schools respond to unacceptable behaviour in pupils. A 'system of dialogue' has been proposed as an approach to support pupils who are persistently punished to meet regularly with staff and reflect on their behaviour, understand why it is unacceptable and learn how to behave more respectfully. A 'system of dialogue' can improve your understanding of pupils who are frequently punished, enhance your relationships with them and help develop more effective ways of improving behaviour in pupils who misbehave. Guidance has been provided to help you work with staff and pupils to encourage children to use their voice, make positive changes to their school culture and instil a greater sense of justice. Strategies of how you can develop more harmonious relationships between schools and marginalized families have also been outlined.

Chapter 5

Professional Development for School Practitioners

Designing and Implementing Staff Training on Bullying

Introduction

Background

Although schools have a legal duty to tackle bullying it is not compulsory for teachers to be trained on how to do so and there is not clear guidance about what should be included in this training. Being legally obliged to resolve such a serious problem which you have not had training for can place you, your pupils and colleagues in an extremely vulnerable position. This chapter will show you how to provide training for staff to understand the complexity of school bullying and develop strategies to combat its multi-faceted nature. Such an approach includes bullying between pupils, staff and pupils, and systemic bullying. How to deal with bullying between colleagues will also be outlined. Guidance will also be provided to help you to enhance the understanding and resources of pupils and staff to combat bullying.

What you can do

If your school does not provide training about bullying you could offer to help them design and deliver staff training on school bullying. You might ask your manager if you can collaborate with a team of colleagues to enhance understanding of bullying and what to do about it. Your senior management team may provide training on bullying, and if not, you could request that they do. If your school is resistant to training provision on bullying and you are a trade union officer you can provide training for union members, and find out if non-union members can also participate in the training. Alternatively, you can arrange for an external expert to provide the training. I currently provide training in tackling complex cases of bullying. Such provision has received excellent feedback from various organizations, for example:

> A good presentation with interesting research being shared; this is something I could use when talking with trainee teachers about how to support pupils who are being bullied; or display bullying behaviour. Every school needs an Elizabeth Nassem! (Teacher trainer)

> Informative, well delivered, and will prove to be really useful in my future practice. (Trainee teacher)

> The day exceeded our expectations and the feedback from the event has shown a real appetite for organizations and individuals to work together to tackle the cultural and structural causes of bullying over the long term. (Consultant surgeon)

The following section explains how staff can be trained to understand the complexity of school bullying.

Researching the problem

My doctoral and post-doctoral research and interventions provide the foundations of knowledge upon which the continuing professional development (CPD) discussed in this chapter is based. To identify and resolve the specific issues of bullying in your school you can conduct research on a smaller scale and share your findings in the staff training you facilitate. Review your school's anti-bullying policy and ensure that you know about associated policies and behavioural frameworks such as your school's behavioural policy and e-safety policy. Ask pupils and staff in focus groups the following core questions:

- What experiences of bullying do children have?
- What is usually done about bullying?
- How should bullying be dealt with?

You may want to expand on the question about children's experiences of bullying by asking, 'What aspects of bullying particularly concern you?' Explore what forms of bullying individuals mention and if they are more concerned about face-to-face bullying or cyberbullying. Have separate focus groups for pupils and staff so they can speak more openly and confidentially. The response you get to these core questions and the knowledge you gain from reading your school's anti-bullying policy (and associated policies) will provide invaluable content which can help you identify the key priorities to cover in the training you provide.

If you are going to implement an anti-bullying intervention and/or some of the strategies in this book, meet with pupils, colleagues and parents to introduce them to the initiative so they are all aware of it from the beginning. This can be an opportunity for you to ask colleagues, parents and pupils if they want to be part of a core team to participate in designing, implementing and evaluating an intervention. It is particularly advantageous for pupils to have input into developing the training you provide. This will ensure that your understanding of bullying and strategies for tackling it are informed by children's lived experiences. Pupils could help you design and implement the training by highlighting what the most important areas are to address and contribute to part of the training where they teach staff about their experiences of bullying and make recommendations of what would help resolve the problem. If you are implementing a pupil-led intervention you can inform colleagues about this process and what you are learning in the staff training.

Introducing the training
Learning objectives
The training sessions I give on 'The complexity of school bullying and what to do about it' usually last about an hour but have lasted up to three hours and can be expanded to a session for the whole day. See Appendix 4 for a presentation outline on this topic which you might want to deliver. To introduce the training explain the purpose of the session and provide a summary of what will be covered. I explain that the session aims to understand the nuances involved in bullying and develop effective strategies to resolve these issues. I describe how the session will address what constitutes bullying, why children engage in bullying and what interventions have been used to tackle bullying and will reflect on how participants can adapt these strategies to their role. I usually explain the importance of supporting staff to develop the resources necessary to combat bullying and ensure they feel confident to deal with it in all forms, as specified by Ofsted (2012).

Below is an example of aims and objectives of a session.

Aim:

- To enhance understanding of the complexity of bullying and develop effective strategies to reduce it.

Objectives:

- Recognize what constitutes bullying.

- Understand why children engage in bullying.

- Learn about evidence-based approaches to tackle bullying.

- Consider what anti-bullying strategies you can apply and develop in your role.

What is bullying?

Begin the session by asking, 'What is bullying?' Some participants may discuss characteristics associated with bullying such as name-calling and when individuals are ostracized. Or they may refer to the traditional definition that bullying is repeated, intentional and that there must be a clear power imbalance (Olweus 1993). If there are discrepancies between what colleagues consider bullying to be, highlight how individuals perceive bullying differently and that there is no universally agreed or legal definition of bullying (Chan 2009). Critically discuss the dimensions of the traditional approach such as the notion that bullying needs to be repeated. Ask participants how they would feel if a colleague punched them in the face, only once, and had not been physically aggressive to them since. Find out if they would they still feel frightened and/or intimidated by the perpetrator. This can highlight the psychological side-effects of maltreatment which may occur long after the maltreatment. Discuss whether an act of aggression has to be repeated to constitute bullying.

Outline what your school's definition of bullying is. If there are discrepancies between your school's definition of bullying and that of colleagues, you might want to revisit your school's definition of bullying. Discuss how the traditional approach aims to clearly distinguish what experiences of maltreatment are bullying from those which are not. However, I explain that bullying involves a spectrum of maltreatment which ranges from mild to severe and causes distress to others, and that there are many 'grey' areas. There are also different modalities of bullying such as: bullying between pupils, bullying between pupils and teachers, and systemic bullying.

To emphasize the nuances and the importance of understanding how individuals perceive their behaviour ask colleagues, 'Is teasing bullying?' Participants usually say that this depends on how the recipient feels and their relationship with the person who is taunting them; for example, they might be friends with them and not feel hurt by the comments. However, some participants have been hurt by being teased, even by their friends. Explain how individuals can attempt to avoid taking responsibility for bullying by saying 'I didn't mean it' or 'We were only joking'. Consider how it can be difficult to establish with certainty whether people are upset by teasing because individuals may conceal their hurt feelings. To learn how to investigate whether bullying is present within the 'grey' areas, ask participants to discuss the following two case studies.

Case Study: Friendship Disputes or Bullying?

In a small Year 6 class there are ten pupils (three girls and seven boys). The three girls, Tanya, Emily and Maria, have persistent arguments and conflict with one another almost every day they attend school. Tanya tells her teacher, Mrs Walker, that she feels upset and torn by her friends Maria and Emily who are both vying for her attention but do not want to be friends with one another; for example, Tanya wants to sit with both her friends but Maria does not want to sit with Emily. However, Maria told Mrs Walker that she felt upset and angry with Tanya and Emily because they always make her feel left out and Tanya always sits with Emily. After persistently having to resolve disputes between the girls, Mrs Walker says to them, 'Tell me when you stop arguing, girls, cos Tanya feels like the piggy in the middle.' There had previously been an incident when the girls had been to swimming lessons at school, and Maria and Tanya hid Emily's knickers, which they said was for a joke. However, Emily was upset by this incident as she went home without wearing her underwear and her mum complained to the school.

- Who is bullying whom or is it nothing to worry about?
- Would you investigate the underlying issues which are contributing to the conflict and whether there is bullying?
- If you investigate this matter further, what do you need to find out?
- What could Mrs Walker do to help resolve this conflict?

There does not seem to be a clear power imbalance in this case study but you can talk further with participants about this, and consider where the power imbalance might be. Discuss how you can empower children who feel entrapped within their unhealthy relationships to interact with each other more respectfully. The case study could also be used to talk about how children may desire to affiliate with certain children in a group but may not want to interact with the other group members, and consider when this might constitute bullying.

Case Study: Play-Fighting or Bullying?

A group of boys play a game, nearly every break and lunch-time, where the popular boys chase the boys who are less popular, such as Edward. As part of the game, the boys hit Edward with sticks and tell him to sit in the bin or they will put him in the bin. Consequently, Edward sits in the bin, is whipped and gets red marks over his body.

- Is this bullying, violence or just a game?
- How might this behaviour appear to teachers if they observe it at playtime? Would it look like bullying or a game?
- How can you find out if Edward is voluntarily playing the game?
- Is Edward coerced or forced into playing the game?
- Why might Edward go along with the game and not report it to you?
- What further information do you need to know?

Why do children bully?

It is important to understand why children engage in bullying. If you facilitate focus groups with pupils before the training session, address why children bully. These findings can be incorporated into your training with anonymous quotations from children. I always discuss the main themes which have emerged from my research about why children bully; these are: to achieve social power by being popular; because they are jealous of a particular attribute their target has; because they are being bullied; and to relieve boredom. Furthermore, children feel coerced into reinforcing societal inequalities inherent in school whereby the 'vulnerable', such as children with learning difficulties, are susceptible to victimization (Nassem 2017). There is an argument that children engage in bullying because they observe others doing so and receive regular rewards for bullying, as implied by Bandura, Ross and Ross (1961). However, I explain that individuals are not just a product of their environment; there are individual differences and children can exercise agency by not engaging in bullying.

Different forms of bullying

Discuss the different forms of bullying such as cyberbullying, homophobia and racist bullying.

Cyberbullying

If you have spoken to pupils prior to the training about their experiences of online bullying this will help ensure your information about cyberbullying is current and directly applies to them. The cyberbullying of pupils is often a continuation of face-to-face bullying; it creates few new victims, but is mainly a tool to harm victims already bullied by traditional means (Wolke, Lee and Guy 2017), although in some cases, the identity of the perpetrator might not be known to the person who is victimized online, and what is placed on the internet can remain permanently (Kyriacou and Zuin 2015). If people think that they are not going to be identified online they may be more likely to be more unpleasant. McAfee (2013) found that only 23 per cent of children who had directed cruel or abusive language to someone online considered it as 'mean' and only 9 per cent acknowledged it as cyberbullying.

I have found that children in primary school were usually more concerned with face-to-face bullying than online bullying (Nassem 2018). However, a few children I have recently interviewed in secondary school have reported that they would like adults to be more informed about how much their communication is online and how prevalent bullying can be through technology. They felt pressured to have lots of friends on social networking websites and to communicate frequently online as otherwise it might look like they have 'no friends'. Throughout this process some children might experience others posting mean comments about them.

Ask children about where they experience or witness cyberbullying before the staff training so you can include this information in your training material. Children bullied online might receive threats and violent images. Advise staff to keep up to date with the forms of technology through which children are experiencing bullying. Ask staff about the ways in which children are bullied online and consider their response in relation to what children have told you about their experiences of cyberbullying. In my recent research in Carfield Primary Academy I found that although staff thought pupils were being bullied on WhatsApp, pupils felt bullying was more prevalent through gaming. Based on the feedback from staff you might decide that this is an area where more training provision is required to keep up to date about cyberbullying.

Homophobic and transphobic bullying

Approximately half of lesbian, gay, bisexual and transgender (LGBT) pupils are bullied for being LGBT in British schools. Eighty-six per cent of pupils hear the phrases 'that's so gay' or 'you're so gay' in school (Stonewall 2017). To help educate colleagues, explain how the use of the word 'gay' in a pejorative sense constitutes homophobic language and this can have serious consequences for individuals who engage in it; for example, employees can be dismissed from their job for this behaviour. Discuss how you can work with colleagues and pupils together to challenge group norms which target children who are LGBT. It has been discussed in Chapter 2 that children who are lesbian, gay or bisexual are more likely to be bullied by groups rather than individuals (Rivers and Cowie 2006).

Stonewall (2014) have found that 27 per cent of transgender people have attempted suicide. Consider with colleagues the issues transgender pupils might have in school and how school can be more inclusive. Reflect with participants about how you can challenge norms that reinforce gender stereotypes both individually and collectively. To enhance inclusivity, ask colleagues to avoid unnecessary gendered language and using gender as a way to divide individuals. You could have a gender-neutral uniform and you don't have to directly state what uniform is for males and females. If you have a transgender young person/people in school you could ask them how they would like the matter to be addressed and if they would like to have input into enhancing knowledge and support about the issue. Support transgender pupils with responses to questions they are likely to be asked by other pupils such as whether they are male or female. Despite the progress of the LGBT movement, current research indicates that much more work still needs to be done to accept and include individuals who are LGBT.

Sexual bullying

Discuss issues of sexual bullying between pupils, and between pupils and staff. Speaking with pupils before the training session is held about their experiences of sexual bullying will help frame your discussion. In my research, children told that me that some girls, such as girls who are popular, can get called 'slags'. I have also described how a girl thought her male teacher always looked up girls' skirts and so she always wore trousers. As a teacher I have experienced sexual comments from pupils about my physical appearance. I have not received any training on how to respond to these comments and these issues were never discussed with colleagues. Consequently, I felt uncomfortable talking to them about my experiences and unsure of how to respond. Some female pupils have recently informed me that they have been called names such as 'frigid' and boys have suggested that they have plastic surgery on their breasts to make them larger or smaller. However, boys have told me that they have felt pressured to be hyper-masculine and can be victimized if they do not engage in gender stereotyped behaviour.

Discuss with colleagues the parameters of what behaviours are sexually appropriate and inappropriate and where you should establish boundaries. Consider with participants how to respectfully inform pupils and staff that their behaviours are sexually inappropriate. From this dialogue you can develop guidance and examples of what constitutes sexually inappropriate behaviours and how to respond. If further issues arise from this discussion you may want to do more research into developing effective approaches to understand and address the issues of sexual bullying. You can also work more with external agencies, such as the police, to enhance your support.

Bullying between pupils and teachers

Ask colleagues how teachers and pupils communicate with one another and when conflict can arise. Once you have had this conversation discuss how teachers can bully, and be bullied by, pupils. Reflect on what might contribute to bullying between pupils and teachers such as pressures on teachers to ensure students are achieving at the expected academic standards. Consider what behaviours staff might inadvertently engage in which pupils might role-model, such as humiliating other pupils and being sarcastic. Reflect upon the 'grey' areas, for example, when sarcasm becomes bullying and the difference between effective discipline and bullying. This will help you clarify what behaviours are acceptable and unacceptable. Ask colleagues about the circumstances in which pupils might bully their teachers. Discuss what might make staff vulnerable to bullying by pupils and find out what support colleagues require to deal with bullying by pupils. Following this, you can look further into developing strategies to prevent bullying between teachers and pupils. You might want to incorporate information and examples of what you have learned about bullying between pupils and staff in the staff training into your school's anti-bullying policy.

Bullying between colleagues

If we want to encourage staff to consistently interact respectfully with pupils then they should also be treated respectfully by colleagues and senior managers. Investigate whether staff feel they are spoken to respectfully by colleagues and school leaders. Ask staff if they have ever felt bullied by colleagues, how they have been bullied and if they feel they can challenge the bullying. Some teachers have told me that some staff speak to them aggressively and they have felt under immense pressure for students to achieve highly in their assessments. You can delve further into these issues of workplace bullying and consider the difference between effective staff management and bullying. In a training session I provided I asked participants if they had experienced bullying more online or offline in their workplace. They said they experienced more bullying offline. Their experience of online bullying was usually from their colleagues through emails, for example, when lots of people were copied into emails when the information in the email was demeaning and they subsequently felt humiliated. To enhance your understanding of this matter, ask colleagues how they are bullied online. If bullying is prevalent through emails, discuss how this is experienced and can be dealt with. Ask staff if they have any recommendations for how to support staff who may feel bullied. I advise staff to seek informal resolution with the person who is causing them distress before they make an official complaint. Encourage colleagues to explain to the person who is bullying them what has happened which has upset them, how it is affecting them and request that the maltreatment stop. However, in some cases, for example when bullying is particularly profound, this dialogue may not be helpful as victimized individuals might feel too intimidated. Staff can make an informal grievance within their grievance policy to encourage their problem to be taken seriously. Once an informal complaint has been made it can escalate into a formal complaint. I advise all staff to be a member of a trade union so they can have representation and support. Advise staff to keep a record of incidents and witnesses. The case study below can stimulate discussion and reflection in a training session which covers workplace bullying.

Case Study: Workplace Bullying

Christina lodged a formal complaint about her manager, Phoebe, who belittled her, spread unpleasant gossip about her and made a formal complaint about her capability to do her work. Phoebe claimed that Christina had not done a large project which she had actually completed (and Christina had evidence that she had done so). Christina was concerned that her manager made a formal complaint about her work performance rather than checking she had done the task. Several of Christina's colleagues had also spread gossip about her and complained to her manager about her work performance and 'unprofessional' behaviour. In the investigation, Christina felt that only Phoebe's friends were interviewed who had all bullied her by undermining and ostracizing her. All of the staff who were interviewed stated that they did not think that Phoebe bullied Christina, and Christina's complaint was not upheld. After the investigation, Phoebe accused Christina of bullying her and used her 'friends' as witnesses to support her complaint.

- How common do you think this outcome is? Why has it happened?

- What can Christina do? What can she ask to be done if she appeals against the procedure of the investigation?

- What would you do if you were accused of being a bully? How might you respond to the person who has accused you?

The majority of reports about bullying in the workplace are not adequately addressed (Mackridge 2018), although it is becoming more common for complaints to be partially upheld. In some cases, individuals who are in conflict can both lodge complaints about each other because hostility has developed over a period of time and relationships have broken down. It will be worthwhile to address issues of bullying in the early stages to improve the chance that the issues can be resolved informally rather than allowing bullying to escalate. Individuals can appeal about the outcome of an investigation which is not upheld within a period of time specified by the organization and can ask for certain witnesses to be interviewed.

Being accused of bullying can be an extremely stressful and isolating process. Inform staff that if they feel comfortable and that it is appropriate, they can speak calmly to the person who feels bullied by them to find out what the problem is and how it might be resolved. Advise them to be calm, listen to why they feel bullied and consider how they can redress this issue. To prevent conflict from escalating, ensure that their lines of communication are clear with colleagues and if they are unsure of instructions then they should seek clarification. Staff should seek clear and unambiguous communication with colleagues and clarity of what is expected in their role. Some of the strategies in this book such as 'Mentoring for "Bullies"' can be adopted to help address bullying between colleagues and the pupil-led approaches can be adopted to become person-centered approaches.

Staff training on systemic bullying

Discuss systemic bullying and what this consists of. Address how issues of social class, learning difficulties/disabilities and gender inequalities can influence how children experience and engage in bullying. Talk about what factors might make certain groups susceptible to bullying and why this might happen. Consider with colleagues why children with learning difficulties/disabilities are more likely to be bullied. Ask why certain groups such as working-class males with learning difficulties are more likely to be in trouble for bullying rather than children who are succeeding academically, perceived as obedient and popular. Encourage participants to reflect on what they can do to tackle bullying which can target children from marginalized groups.

Talk about whether colleagues think systems of punishment in your school are fair. Ask if certain individuals are being persistently punished and if the punishment is improving their behaviour. Address with participants how they think systems of punishment can be developed to help pupils improve their behaviour. I recommend having a 'system of dialogue' to speak regularly with children who misbehave to understand that their behaviour is unacceptable and for staff to find the underlying reasons for the behaviour. A mentoring programme can help improve a child's understanding of what behaviours cause harm to others and learn how they can improve their behaviour. Consider with colleagues what alternative means the school can use to instil a greater sense of justice into their culture.

Discuss issues around protected characteristics. For example, ask colleagues if they think aspects of the schooling system such as streaming can marginalize children with learning difficulties, and cause hostilities and divisions between them and the children in the higher streams. Consider with colleagues if there is anything that you can do as a team to address these issues. Of course, there are systemic inequalities entrenched in school which as an individual you are unlikely to change. However, it is important to address what aspects of unfairness in school you can support colleagues to improve.

Racial bullying

Loach and Bloor (1995) argue that racism experienced by adults is usually considered as bullying when it involves children. Racism in this book is considered as a form of bullying associated with systemic inequalities. If you facilitate a focus group about children's experiences of bullying prior to providing staff training, ask them about how children experience racial bullying in your school. In Carfield Primary

Academy (CPA) I provided a pupil-led intervention with Muslim children where most of the children's ethnic origin was from Pakistan. These children told me that they had experienced name-calling because of the colour of their skin, in many cases by children who were the same ethnicity as them. This bullying was associated with having a different skin colour which was considered as too light or too dark, depending on how the perpetrators perceived the child:

> Taaliq: They bully you for no reason, for bad reasons, like the colour of your skin…
> Yana: It's like saying black, black, black.
> Aalia: Not only if you're dark, if you're light-skinned, if you're fair-skinned.
> Taaliq: It depends which person you're bullying… Someone who is light-skinned, they will target the people who are brown and black, but if there's someone who is black then they're targeting people who are white and brown.
> Sunita: Some people don't bully kids for their skin colour, sometimes for their religion.
>
> (Second focus group, Year 5, CPA)

The Muslim children I interviewed had been called names such as 'terrorist' because of their religion. Sunita reported, 'My friend texted me and she said, 'look, you're a terrorist':

> Taaliq: If you tell the teacher you kind of feel embarrassed to tell the teacher because you don't know, she probably thinks that as well in her head. You get dirty looks on the streets as well.
> Aalia: It makes me feel really ashamed.
> Taaliq: It makes you feel embarrassed. It makes you ashamed of who you are.
>
> (Second focus group, Year 5, CPA)

The bullying that these children experienced made them feel ashamed and embarrassed because they thought they were perceived negatively by others and even felt that even their teachers might perceive them as inferior because of their religion. Aalia (Year 5, CPA) said that it was unfair that Muslims are being blamed for crimes that they have not committed: 'It's not like we're doing it. We don't say that to someone. It's just harsh.' Taaliq (Year 5, CPA) explained that terrorism is against Muslim beliefs: 'In Islam, if they are real Muslims, well, they're not any more, because in Islam you're not allowed to kill someone. It's not up to you when their life gets taken, it's up to God.'

To address racial bullying, find out what the issues are in your school and speak to colleagues and pupils to learn how you can address it. Talking about children's problems and listening to them can be the most effective first steps to tackle the issues. Raise awareness for all pupils about what racial bullying consists of, and the legal consequences there can be for perpetrators of racism.

You can help children reflect on how they can respond internally and externally to perpetrators of racism. For example, ask if negative comments about an individual's skin colour, religion or physical appearance constitute bullying. Ask children who experience such negative comments: how does it make you feel, why have they said it, how can you make yourself not get too distressed and offended, how can you perceive yourself in a more positive light, and finally, how can you respond in a way that deals with the problem effectively?

How can teachers help?

There are high expectations of teachers to prevent and tackle bullying. Chan (2009) considers teachers to be social engineers of change in the classroom. Ask teachers to what extent they can influence children to change. Some teachers may feel they can help children make a lot of positive changes but some may feel quite limited. Discuss how staff can support children to make improvements and what restrictions they might have in dealing with bullying. Find out if colleagues feel confident and equipped to tackle bullying in your school, as Ofsted (2012) recommends. If colleagues do not feel confident to do so, ask what support they require to help them.

Raise the issue that pupils may not report being bullied and ask participants why this might be the case. Participants usually say that children are afraid that their bullying will increase if they report it and they might feel too ashamed to admit they are being bullied. If you receive this feedback then reflect with colleagues on how effective your school is at responding to bullying. Address how you can develop a culture which encourages children to talk more openly to staff if they are being bullied. To encourage pupils to open up about bullying you could explain that bullying affects everyone. To avoid children feeling stigmatized for bullying or being victimized I remind participants that I consider bullying as a spectrum of characteristics associated with bullying (such as ostracism and teasing) which ranges from mild to severe rather than aiming to clearly categorize which children are 'bullies' and 'victims'. Advise staff to involve the child who is victimized in deciding how their bullying will be dealt with. I highlight the importance of teachers dealing with conflict in class when it occurs and agreeing the ground rules of how pupils and staff will interact with one another respectfully in the first lessons they have with pupils, and reinforcing this throughout the academic year.

Ask participants, 'How can you help a child if you think they are being bullied but they don't report it to you?' I inform staff that if they think a child is being bullied they should speak with them after class and ask how they are. You could mention what behaviours you have noticed they have been experiencing from other pupils that have led to your enquiry and ask them how they feel. Children may not confide in you immediately but you could ask them after a week or so about how they are getting along and monitor the situation. You might want to speak with other people who are involved to find out more about what is happening.

Advise participants how to investigate bullying. This consists of speaking to all the pupils involved in the bullying. In your investigation find out what people think about the incident and how they feel about it, as well as finding out what they witnessed. Discuss how you can arrange to speak with children after the investigation to check the bullying has not reoccurred. I advise staff to be vigilant to signs and symptoms of bullying which should be specified in your anti-bullying policy. These symptoms include anxiety; developing a stammer; being socially withdrawn; and under-performance in work. One major symptom I have noticed is that a victimized child is often ostracized, persistently blamed for incidents and it can appear that no one likes them. However, some of these symptoms could be because of other problems such as family conflict so it is important to speak with the individuals involved to find out if bullying is present. If pupils don't feel comfortable reporting bullying, find out why and work with colleagues to investigate how you can improve your school's approach to reporting and addressing bullying.

Activity: discussion using news reports
Details of news reports
Present participants with two news reports about bullying which have different perspectives of bullying as case studies to discuss. I have used a report from BBC News (News Report 1) showing that childhood anxiety and depression caused by childhood bullying declines with

time. Anxiety and depression found in over 11,000 twins (aged 11, 14 and 16) was present two years after the bullying but had disappeared after five years (BBC News 2017). The researchers conclude that their research shows children are able to recover from bullying. I also used a news report from *The Independent* (News Report 2) about a schoolboy, Louie Fenton, aged 12, who was found hanged after bullies threw meat at him because he was vegan. He had been forced to eat outside, had had regular appointments with the counsellor and had started self-harming (*The Independent* 2017).

Discussion
Ask the participants to read the two newspaper articles. After they have read the reports ask them to work in pairs or small groups of about four to discuss the reports and the following questions. Ask them to include any additional thoughts that are relevant which they would like to contribute.

News Report 1: Anxiety and depression declines after bullying

- Why might anxiety have declined with time?
- To what extent do you think bullying is associated with mental health problems?
- Does bullying cause mental health problems or does having a mental health problem contribute to not coping well with bullying?
- How can schools lessen the side-effects of bullying through supporting the mental health of children?

News Report 2: Suicide

- How might the children who threw the meat at Louie explain their behaviour?
- How much do you think bullying contributed to Louie's suicide? What else might have contributed to it?
- There was an open coroner's verdict which means that the death is judged to be suspicious but no other verdict had been confirmed. Why do you think there was an open coroner's verdict?
- How could you find out what the school did about the bullying?

News Reports 1 and 2

- One news report shows how bullying is associated with suicide and one shows that anxiety declines with time. Which one do you think is more convincing? Explain why you have reached your decision.

- Which news report (1 or 2) do you have the most reservations about and why?

Additional Questions

- What role do schools and teachers have in tackling bullying?

- How might pupils be affected by witnessing children being bullied?

- How can we ensure school staff deal with bullying effectively?

Anti-bullying policies and good practice
Department for Education recommendations

Discuss the Department for Education (2017) recommendations for bullying. I usually emphasize how schools will not be marked down by Ofsted for having bullying, rather Ofsted will focus on what has been done about the bullying. To recap, the Department for Education (2017) recommend that pupils are aware of how to report bullying and that the school makes it easy for pupils to report bullying. They advise that parents should be aware of procedures to tackle bullying and that they should feel confident to report bullying. They also recommend working with the wider community to combat bullying collectively. Talk about how you can maximize your involvement with the wider school community in tackling bullying. Emphasize that children should feel that disciplinary measures are consistent, and that incidents are also monitored consistently. Encourage staff to participate in further training and development on bullying to equip them to deal with the complex cases which can arise and ensure their knowledge is current. Encourage colleagues to establish a forum to support each other to deal with bullying such as a pupil and staff ABAG. Speaking to pupils regularly about their experiences of bullying and recommendations of how it should be dealt with will also help to keep your knowledge up to date.

Your school's anti-bullying policy

To enhance your understanding of your school's anti-bullying policy, discuss it with your line managers, colleagues and union representative. Training for staff on bullying can be used to ensure all colleagues are aware of your school's anti-bullying policy. Advise staff to read their anti-bullying policy prior to your session and discuss it with their colleagues to ensure they understand it. In the training you provide, refer to your school's anti-bullying policy and your school's definition of bullying. Most schools refer to the traditional definition of bullying in their anti-bullying policy. Your school's anti-bullying policy is likely to specify the different forms of bullying such as physical and verbal bullying. It should explain how children can report bullying and how bullying will be addressed in school. Children who engage in bullying are usually punished. For example, they may have their playtimes stopped, or be excluded from school for a specified period of time; in more serious cases they may be excluded from school permanently.

Your policy should also specify how you can help children who engage in bullying to improve their behaviour and support those who are victimized. The anti-bullying policy should state how incidents of bullying will be monitored and provide guidance on when parents and the police should be informed. Perhaps you could ask colleagues for feedback about your school's anti-bullying policy. You might want to ask colleagues if there is anything additional which ought to be included in the policy, and if there is anything in the policy that they would like to challenge. Agree how you will review and update your school's current anti-bullying policy, and seek feedback from colleagues, pupils and parents.

Established strategies for tackling bullying between pupils

Traditional approaches to tackling bullying include increasing supervision in unsupervised areas where bullying is likely to occur such as toilets (Boulton 1994). Creating a stimulating environment can also help diminish boredom which may reduce bullying. Discussing bullying at circle time can encourage more openness about bullying and help more children to report bullying (Sullivan 2001). Having anti-bullying assemblies on bullying designed and delivered by pupils is also likely to help combat bullying. In the training you provide, ask participants what aspects of handling bullying they would like to know more about so they can be incorporated into a following session at a later date.

Outline which current approaches are used to tackle bullying. I usually discuss peer support methods such as the shared concern approach (Pikas 1989) which focuses on working primarily with peers including victimized children and perpetrators to resolve the problem. Some schools train a group of pupils to become anti-bullying ambassadors who help address bullying. However, peers must work with the staff and the school community to make significant changes to how bullying is dealt with. Mediation focuses on an adult working with all parties to find solutions. However, pupils may feel their bullying has not been dealt with adequately because perpetrators do not have consequences for their behaviour. Individuals who are bullied may also feel too intimidated to sit in the same room as the person who is bullying them, even though it is usually conducted in a supervised environment. Consequently, it will be worthwhile to encourage colleagues to consider how to help prepare victims and perpetrators for this meeting.

Explain how assertiveness training can be used for perpetrators and victimized children to improve the way they communicate clearly and confidently without appearing aggressive or intimidated. Restorative justice focuses on having structured communication with the individuals directly involved in the bullying to discuss the problems, how they were affected by the incident and what needs to happen to repair the harm. However, restorative justice and assertiveness training focus on changing how individuals respond to others rather than dealing with the underlying issues which contribute to bullying.

Consulting with children
Training to mentor 'bullies'
In the training I deliver to staff I discuss the mentoring I provide for children who persistently engage in bullying. I explain how none of the children in my research have identified themselves as 'bullies'. The purpose of mentoring is to help children who engage in bullying reflect upon how their behaviour causes harm to others, deal with the underlying causes of the behaviour, and learn more respectful ways of interacting with pupils and staff. Speaking with students about what happened, the likely consequences of their actions, how they could respond more respectfully next time and role-playing alternative scenarios can all help break the pattern of negative behaviour (Nassem 2018). I advise participants to provide regular sessions of mentoring to

resolve bullying proactively, rather than reacting to specific incidents afterwards. Mentoring can be expanded to involve those who are in conflict with the mentee and bringing them together into dialogue after several mentoring session have been provided to help resolve the problems. Throughout this process they can explain why they are behaving the way they are and how they feel, and can agree on how they will interact with one another more respectfully in future.

Training on pupil-led approaches

Advise staff to consult with children about their experiences of bullying – and seek recommendations from them of how bullying should be resolved. Ask staff to encourage pupils to reflect on why people are upsetting them in order to understand their perspective. Through consultations with pupils, staff can support pupils to talk about how they feel and reflect on how they can react to hurtful interactions more productively, rather than becoming extremely angry or upset.

Explain how staff can provide children with a diary. Diaries can provide children with an emotional outlet to reflect on their behaviour and thoughts and feelings. Pupil-led sessions with diaries have helped children react to conflict calmly rather than angrily (Nassem 2018). If you are implementing a pupil-led initiative, inform staff in this training session that you are doing so. To help you start a pupil-led intervention, ask colleagues in the training session for ideas about what issues of bullying you can focus on and ask if they want to be involved in this initiative.

Training on 'healthy relationships' with pupils and staff

Emphasize that teachers and students must work together to combat bullying. If you have implemented a pupil-led initiative, children who have been closely involved in it could meet with selected staff such as the head of pastoral care, their class/form teacher and learning mentors to show what they have learnt and feedback their recommendations of how the school can improve the way they respond to bullying. Some of these recommendations could become incorporated into your school's strategy for handling bullying, about which you can provide training to colleagues.

The staff training outlined in this chapter can help pupils and staff to develop healthier relationships with one another. Encourage colleagues to support children to improve their behaviour and help them if their problematic behaviour reoccurs. Advise them to consistently speak to children respectfully, listen to children, respond to their views and take time to understand their perspectives. Pupils are then more likely to do the same with their peers. Reflect with colleagues on which strategies you have suggested which they feel they could use and adapt to their role. Support colleagues to apply the strategies you have taught them to their role so they can resolve the specific cases of bullying they are confronted with.

Post Training

The following section provides recommendations on how you can continue to develop your colleagues' and pupils' understanding of bullying and resources to tackle it after the initial training session provided.

A shared understanding of bullying

The information you receive from participants from the training you deliver, both during and afterwards, can be used to help develop your school strategy for tackling bullying and improve your school's anti-bullying policy. You could investigate in more depth how pupils and colleagues perceive bullying and define bullying. Your findings from this enquiry can be used to enhance your school's definition and understanding of bullying so your school has a shared definition of bullying which applies to your pupils' specific experiences of maltreatment.

Staff development through pupil and staff ABAGs

Collaborating with a team of colleagues in the staff ABAG will strengthen one another's resources in resolving bullying. In the ABAG meetings identify areas relating to bullying which you would like to understand more about so you can effectively resolve the issues. Facilitate problem-solving sessions with colleagues to provide a useful forum to address particularly complex issues about the bullying in your school so you can decide the most effective strategies to deal with them. In these meetings discuss issues such as how to improve your school's approach to tackling bullying, and how you can draw on the child's voice to improve this. Consider how staff can work with children and the pupil ABAG to develop pupil-led approaches. Children's feedback on how bullying is dealt with and recommendations on how it should be resolved could be provided and analysed in the pupil and staff ABAGs to enhance the input children have in developing school strategies to resolve bullying.

Meet with colleagues after the training session to agree how you are going to communicate and interact respectfully with pupils in future. Colleagues might talk about when they have responded disrespectfully to pupils, for example when a pupil is being aggressive to them. Through openly acknowledging the problem colleagues can learn how to challenge pupils more respectfully. These discussions can help you begin to outline a 'healthy relationships' policy and an anti-bullying policy for pupils and staff.

Embedding learning about bullying into the curriculum

Collaborate with colleagues who are committed to tackling bullying to draw up a plan of how you can embed lessons about bullying for pupils into the curriculum. You can also develop a programme which consists of various topics on bullying for staff training. Some of the sessions could be applied to addressing bullying between colleagues.

Sessions about bullying and how to deal with it can be taught in various lessons. In English children can write stories, poems and speeches about bullying. In Drama children can create and perform plays about bullying and role-play alternative ways of responding to bullying. There are also subjects where you can address systemic bullying such as in History. Lessons about the suffragettes can help raise important issues about gender inequality and how individuals can unite together to resist the power which operates over them. In Religious Studies you could link teaching about power, leadership and influence over others with Jesus, his disciples and the leaders of Jerusalem.

Design a scheme of work to teach pupils about bullying. Colleagues from pastoral care and subject leaders should ideally be involved in designing the scheme of work. Lessons about bullying could be part of PSHE where you teach children about various topics related to bullying over a period of time with about seven sessions provided on a weekly basis. These sessions can consist of the following topics on bullying:

- *Defining and understanding bullying.* Ask pupils and/or staff: what is bullying? Discuss the different ways of defining and understanding bullying. Highlight what the most important factors are in deciding whether someone is bullying, such as characteristics of bullying (e.g. teasing and name-calling), how the recipient perceives the negative behaviour and the relationships these individuals have with one another, for example, whether there is a history of maltreatment.

- *Social power and bullying (such as popularity, and peer pressure to conform to social norms).* Investigate with students/staff why children engage in bullying and the concept of popularity. Discuss what people gain by bullying and why people may admire those who bully. Address why individuals may not challenge bullying. Ask how we can tackle bullying which operates subtly through individuals feeling coerced and pressured to conform. Children who engage in bullying who are popular may experience a loss of social status with their peers if they refrain from bullying. To overcome this, discuss how children can maintain their social power through pro-social means, for example, by encouraging their peers to include ostracized pupils in social activities such as sport games.

- *Social class and bullying.* Cover how inequalities associated with social class may influence how children experience and engage in bullying. Reflect on how class culture can have an impact on how pupils behave and respond. Consider the different behavioural norms of pupils, social pressures and expectations of middle-class girls who are succeeding academically compared with males from deprived backgrounds who have learning difficulties. Talk about how you can work together in your school to challenge inequalities in social class and gender which are associated with bullying.

- *Vulnerability and protected characteristics.* Ask participants what individuals and groups are more likely to experience bullying. You could discuss some of the nine protected characteristics as defined by the Equality Act 2010 (Equality and Human Rights Commission 2018). Explain that, according to the Equality Act 2010 it is unlawful to discriminate against someone because of their: age; disability; race; religion or belief; sex and sexual orientation. It is also unlawful to discriminate against individuals because they are transitioning from one gender to another; are legally married or in civil partnership (in employment only); or are pregnant or on maternity leave. Examine with children how individuals who belong to these groups might be susceptible to bullying and experience it differently. Discuss how children can experience sexual bullying in school. Have debates about discrimination, for example discuss whether gender-neutral toilets may make females feel vulnerable but may be more inclusive for transgender pupils, and what might be done to help resolve this issue. Following this session, collaborate with volunteers to establish an equalities group of pupils and staff who meet regularly to discuss and combat discrimination in school.

- *Resolving bullying.* The topic of resolving bullying could be separated into various sections which address previous approaches to resolve it, including your school's approach and pupil-led approaches.

- *Bullying between pupils and teachers.* In this session address how teachers can bully their pupils, and how pupils can bully their teachers. Discuss in depth the difference between bullying and effective classroom management. Ask participants to make recommendations of how to protect staff and pupils from being bullied by one another.

- *'Healthy relationships'.* This session could help lay the foundations for developing a 'healthy relationships' strategy throughout the entire school community, for example with teachers, pupils and learning mentors. Agree what is good practice for how staff and pupils communicate with one another, and how individuals who are in conflict should interact with one another. Emphasize the importance of listening to others and trying to understand one another's perspective. Discuss what systems could be put in place to repair relationships between pupils and staff that have become hostile.

Encourage pupils to research a project on school bullying either individually or as part of a group. Children could investigate the following areas: different forms of bullying; how children who have protected characteristics experience bullying; and how to combat bullying such as anti-bullying interventions and your school's anti-bullying policy. They could then present their research to other pupils and staff. If pupils are advising their peers on what to do about bullying in assemblies or in classroom presentations ensure they are adequately supported to provide helpful advice. Raising awareness about bullying and what to do about it can be particularly helpful in the autumn term as most pupils will have moved up a year group and some children may have moved schools so might feel particularly susceptible to bullying.

Providing additional awareness-raising and support for children who are moving from primary to secondary school is likely to be particularly beneficial to them throughout their transition.

Conclusion

This chapter has provided guidance on how you can provide professional development to colleagues using a multi-faceted model by addressing bullying between pupils, pupils and staff, colleagues, and systemic bullying. An outline has been provided of the content you can use to frame your training sessions along with activities and case studies. Guidance has been included on how you can embed teaching and training about bullying for colleagues and pupils throughout the academic year, for example, through providing lessons on bullying, pupil-led approaches and through engaging with the pupil and staff ABAGs.

Implementing the techniques recommended in this chapter will ensure staff and pupils have an in-depth and broader knowledge base of bullying so they feel more empowered to confront it. Through training school practitioners how to interact more respectfully with colleagues and pupils they will develop healthier relationships. Once you have refined the professional development you provide on school bullying you could invite colleagues from other schools to attend, participate in, and develop further training provision. This will enhance the knowledge, resources and support network in your community to successfully resolve bullying.

Chapter 6

Supporting Children to Combat School Bullying

Initial Design

The pupil-led anti-bullying initiative outlined in this chapter aimed to apply what I had learnt about the complexities of bullying to support pupils and school practitioners in tackling bullying. In particular, it was designed to support those who were victimized in resolving their bullying and help those who engage in bullying to refrain from doing so and behave more respectfully. I also hoped to help school practitioners deal with bullying in a more informed and supportive way, and adhere to safeguarding legislation by ensuring that pupils are protected from harm and are in safe and effective care (DfE 2018).

My approach is different from most other interventions in school bullying such as KiVa because it is tailored to the specific needs of pupils and school practitioners, and pays particular attention to pupil voice. Consequently, it is flexible enough for schools to adjust to pupils' specific experiences of bullying, focuses on developing children's ability to make informed decisions about their behaviour and can be used to deal with the root causes behind the bullying. The anti-bullying initiative was conducted in Hollybrook Academy which is a secondary school in a deprived area in the North of England. Most of the children were white British or British Asian.

When I realized that the school had an anti-bullying co-ordinator, Mrs Shelton, I wasn't sure if the school would feel they needed my support. However, it became apparent that my initiative could be particularly helpful to teachers because dealing with bullying is one of their many duties.

A suite of programmes to support school practitioners and pupils was designed to combat bullying. This included training about what constitutes bullying and how to respond. I asked to meet with school practitioners (such as class teachers, those who worked in pastoral care and heads of years) to improve how they respond to bullying, support them to thoroughly investigate it, and develop action plans and interventions with pupils and staff to embed good practice in the school's culture. I volunteered to establish separate drop-in sessions and 'Bullying: have your say' forums for pupils, parents and staff to share their experiences, to listen to them and help them develop effective strategies to resolve it. Mrs Shelton showed me the bully-boxes around school where children could anonymously report bullying but she did not want me to read the messages. I also proposed to review, update and help communicate the school's anti-bullying policy to children, parents and staff so they would be more fully aware of bullying and what to do about it. I was informed that the school's anti-bullying policy had recently been reviewed and so they did not update them with my suggestions. I also offered to provide mentoring for children who were persistently in trouble for bullying. I wanted to take these children out of isolation and encourage them to reflect on their behaviour to encourage them to 'take responsibility' for their behaviour and develop 'empathetic understanding' towards others. It felt ironic that usually children who needed the most guidance to improve their social skills were often the most marginalized.

Mrs Shelton said she had a list of 'bullies' on a spreadsheet whom, following approval from the pupils' head of year, I could mentor. I was also asked to find a group of pupils who would volunteer to develop a new anti-bullying campaign. For the campaign, Mrs Shelton asked me to make anti-bullying posters and have a poster competition, and write poems with these children. We agreed that I would work in the school for three months to provide mentoring for children who persistently engaged in bullying and lead an anti-bullying campaign with pupils.

In School...

Introductions

I provided an assembly for Year 7 pupils to introduce myself and inform pupils about what constitutes bullying, and what they should do if they were being bullied. I told them about the anti-bullying campaign I would be developing with pupils and that they could speak with me at lunch-time if they wanted to participate in it.

I visited Hollybrook during three lunch-times to find children who wanted to participate in the campaign. When I arrived in the school hall, many children were inquisitive and asked who I was. There were a group of Year 10 girls who sat behind me who were quite loud and were spilling water and throwing food. I introduced myself and told them about the work I was doing, and they said they wanted to be involved in the project. I was also introduced to Zane, who was also in Year 10, by the head of Year 9, Mr Baker, who informed me that Zane would be an ideal person to be involved in the campaign and had recently been behaving very well.

After my lunch-time visits to school I had a list of 20 pupils who were in Years 7 to 10. To implement the anti-bullying campaign, I went into school every other week when pupils had their 'behavioural lesson' which was a non-curriculum lesson when they were catching up on their homework. Six children arrived; four were the Year 10 girls I had met who had been throwing food and spilling drinks, one girl was in Year 7 and Zane was the only boy. The child who was in Year 7 was quiet and came along to the first four sessions. Each child in Year 10 attended most, if not all, the sessions. The Year 10 children were from deprived backgrounds and most of them struggled with their work; they were not traditionally academic. They had behavioural problems and were aggressive to some other pupils and staff. They had difficulties concentrating on their work and I realized that it may have been convenient for teachers to release them from their class.

I started the session by introducing the project and asking children to make posters and write poems about bullying. Children started to share some of their experiences of bullying with the group. When Ava was writing a poem about her experience of bullying, Zane said loudly, 'Ava's not getting bullied, she's the most popularist in school.' However, Ava started to confide in the pupils about her experience of bullying which had upset her immensely. Following Ava's disclosure, other pupils started to share their thoughts and feelings about bullying whilst they were writing poems, speeches and posters. Throughout this process they realized that they had all been profoundly affected by bullying which helped them develop 'empathetic understanding' through learning about the perspectives of others. Pupils took the work seriously, reminded their teachers to release them from class to do the work and the pupils in Year 10 also brought along some of their 'mates' (who also had behavioural problems) to join the group.

Pupil-led assemblies

Mrs Shelton asked if I would support the anti-bullying campaigners to present an assembly for anti-bullying week. The children were enthusiastic and felt honoured by the responsibility they were entrusted with. Mrs Shelton said she was pleased that Zane, who was often in trouble for his behaviour, had a positive outlet to channel his energies into. She was also surprised by how keen the children were to present their work in assembly.

The pupils asked to present their work to Year 7 pupils in assembly since the pupils in Year 10 were worried about being embarrassed and humiliated by children who were older. I supported these pupils to find out what they wanted to say and how they wanted to say it, kept a record of this and co-ordinated the assembly.

All the children arrived at assembly on time, prepared and took their roles very seriously. In assembly, they talked about the effects of bullying, how it had hurt them and advised children what to do if they were being bullied. Megan shared her advice with pupils about what to do if they were being bullied:

> Hello, I am Megan and I am a peer mentor. Peer mentors can help you if you are being bullied so you can talk to your peer mentor if you want help. Bullying is really upsetting and no one should have to be bullied. If you are being bullied you should report it to a teacher and inform your parents. You can report bullying online or you can report it through the bully-boxes. Don't suffer in silence; speak out if you are being bullied!
>
> (Megan, Year 10, Hollybrook Academy)

The anti-bullying campaigners were positive role-models to younger pupils; they challenged normalized practices which enable bullying and tried to make it more acceptable to report it.

Chloe had frequently been reported to teachers for bullying pupils and she was frequently physically violent and verbally abusive to them. However, Chloe had also been bullied by her peers and had also observed members of her family such as her father and cousins respond violently to others. Her involvement in the anti-bullying campaign allowed her to use her experience of bullying others and being victimized to understand how others felt when they were bullied. She explained, 'I used to be in trouble for bullying but I do not want to bully anyone now. Bullying is awful, it makes people feel sad and ruins their lives' (Chloe, Year 10, Hollybrook Academy).

Although Chloe had previously bullied other children she realized how distressing it can be and no longer wanted to continue to do so. She had developed 'empathetic understanding' of the perspectives and feelings of those whom she hurt. Through Chloe's public announcement of her desire to improve her behaviour she rejected being labelled as a 'bully'. She became a positive role-model by showing how pupils can use their power to help others rather than abuse them. Chloe improved how other pupils perceived her and her speech helped staff see her more positively; they developed 'empathetic understanding' of Chloe's struggles and felt inspired by her desire to change. Staff who saw her in assembly and heard what she had said praised Chloe for her courage and desire to change, and told other colleagues about her.

Children who presented their work also felt respected and valued by both pupils and staff, which improved their relationships with them. The pupil-led campaign meant that children took a central role in sharing their views and experiences. This made them feel important and gave them a sense of influence and esteem as they put anti-bullying principles into practice. The anti-bullying campaign implemented the 'take responsibility' strategy where pupils shared their experiences and feelings to support other pupils and address bullying in their school.

Pupils also improved their communication skills as I taught them how to provide more eye contact, speak clearly and more slowly. I also taught pupils how to use pauses and use their facial expressions and body language to articulate their feelings rather than behaving aggressively. Instead of feeling angry because of bullying they felt proud of what they had achieved to help address it.

Second assembly

Enthused by the positive response from the first assembly, children wanted to provide another anti-bullying assembly to pupils in Year 8. Again, children decided what they wanted to say and I gave them guidance on how to present and express themselves and articulate their ideas.

Bullying was a particularly important issue for Zane as he was experiencing homophobic and transphobic bullying, and was repeatedly called abusive names which hurt him and made him feel angry and ostracized. The head of Year 9, Mr Baker, and head of Year 10, Mr Hyde, told me they were concerned about Zane's disruptive and attention-seeking behaviour. Sometimes he retaliated to those who tormented him and was physically aggressive, for example, by throwing chairs at them. The opportunity to express his thoughts and feelings, and perform to an audience about an issue which profoundly affected him, provided Zane with a positive outlet for his emotions and allowed him to achieve attention and respect through positive means. He prepared a speech at home to present in assembly to explain to pupils the damage bullying can cause and read it to his teachers. In his speech which he entitled 'It's all regret in the end!' he said, 'Bullying is a major part of a school life, it happens a lot more than your cells contact your brain, it hurts feelings and breaks hearts; it breaks people' (Zane, Year 10). Zane's speech highlights the destruction to people's lives and emotions that bullying can cause.

As soon as the children had prepared their presentations for assembly and Zane had read his speech to his teachers, the children told me that assembly had been cancelled and they felt extremely disappointed. The teachers confirmed that assembly had been cancelled by Mrs Morris, the head of Year 8, because she was not coming into school that day, and it would be held next term after the campaign had finished.

At the end of my time in school the children whom I had worked with wanted to develop the anti-bullying campaign with new ideas. Zane asked if we could provide an anti-bullying office where a member of staff focuses specifically on supporting children who are being bullied to receive help when they require it. He asked for me to work there permanently and wanted the group to become anti-bullying ambassadors who could then support other pupils who were bullied. However, once the momentum of this campaign had developed, most of the staff involved appeared to become more resistant towards it. In cases where external experts come into a school environment some staff may perceive them as a threat and feel defensive. They may feel concerned that they could be blamed for the issues of bullying in their school, particularly if they have not had adequate training and support to tackle bullying. Consequently, it is important that external provision focuses on supporting staff rather than making them feel exposed and targeted.

'Mentoring for "Bullies"': A Pilot Study
Aims of the programme
I had learnt from researching my doctorate that children who were usually punished by their teachers for bullying other pupils were often those from working-class backgrounds who had learning difficulties. These children were from particularly economically deprived working-class backgrounds. They tended to value approval from their peers rather than obey their teachers. Most of these children were males but there were some females from this socio-economic background who also experienced these forms of bullying. Many of these children felt that being bullied by their peers, and/or picked on by their teachers, had contributed to their aggressive behaviour, which subsequently led

to some of them being excluded from school, either temporarily or permanently. Pupils who had been permanently excluded from school felt that they had ruined their chances in life and were on a downward spiral which they could not stop. I wanted to encourage them to reflect on their behaviour and choices; improve their relationships with their peers and teachers; and learn how to improve their circumstances.

Mrs Shelton told all the heads of years about the mentoring I was available to provide and asked them to refer pupils who were identified as 'bullies' to work with me. Mr Baker (head of Year 9) initially asked me to work with some pupils in his year group. I was later asked by the head of Year 11, Mrs Williams, to work with one of the pupils in her year group, Mark. Mr Baker also occasionally asked me to work with some Year 10 pupils. The mentoring I provided aimed to resolve tensions and conflicts between pupils, and pupils and teachers. I also aimed to implement the 'empathetic understanding' approach by enhancing the mentee's understanding of the perspective of other pupils and staff they had upset, and also support staff to understand the mentee's perspective.

Work undertaken

I initially provided mentoring to pupils individually but as the mentoring developed I sometimes worked with pupils in small groups (between three and six pupils who were in Year 9 and Year 10). In the mentoring on an individual basis support was in depth and tailored more specifically to a pupil's particular requirements. In the mentoring children in groups meant that the group dynamics could be openly discussed as they were being directly experienced. Mentees were mostly males who were in Year 9 who were often in trouble for being physically aggressive to pupils. They were often punished by teachers, felt 'picked on' by them and subsequently responded aggressively towards them. This vicious cycle of teacher–pupil conflict contributed to increasing hostility. For example, when pupils were shouted at by teachers, sometimes they would respond by using abusive language and personal insults which contributed to the teachers shouting more angrily and instilling harsher punishments. It became apparent that pupil–teacher relationships were important areas which needed addressing in the mentoring.

I designed an outline of sessions to cover various topics which aimed to improve the mentee's behaviour. See Appendix 5 for an outline of the mentoring programme which can help you provide individualized support for pupils who persistently engage in bullying. See Appendix 6 for examples of how you can cover sessions of group mentoring for pupils who persistently engage in bullying.

I developed a topic, 'Talking so people listen', which aimed to support mentees to develop skills in peacefully resolving disagreements with their peers and teachers and learn how to receive more positive responses from them. Additional topics covered in these sessions included: choices and consequences, and turning things around. Sessions also focused on helping pupils understand the perspectives of their peers and staff. I helped them understand why teachers may have disciplined them, for example excluding them from class, which enhanced their 'empathetic understanding'. I examined with children what parts of their lives they could change if they wanted to; what aspects of their lives were difficult to change; what behaviours they had engaged in which they had regretted and what they could learn from this; and how they could improve their behaviour in future. We also discussed why they behave in ways that get them into trouble which involved covering topics such as peer pressure.

To support children with their specific lived experiences I asked them to provide a recent example of when they were involved in disagreements with another pupil and/or school practitioner. I analyzed the incident and how they felt by asking questions such as what happened, what they did and what the other person did, and explored their thoughts and feelings throughout this process. I discussed with pupils the likely reactions from others as a consequence of their behaviour. I also drew on the mentee's experiences of how they felt when they were bullied so they could relate to how other pupils and school practitioners felt when they bullied them. Sessions provided an in-depth approach for children to reflect upon, understand and explain their own behaviour.

I encouraged children to express their emotions and understand how their feelings had contributed to their aggressive response. This enhanced our understanding of what motivated them to subject staff and/or pupils to maltreatment. I also provided sessions on communication to encourage children to effectively articulate their feelings and improve their body language. I encouraged them to use more eye contact as I noticed when I met with them that they hardly provided any. I hoped that encouraging children to provide more eye contact would help them to pay attention to and understand the feelings of others, and develop more empathy.

Mentoring aimed to support children to learn what aspects of their lives they could choose and where there were opportunities in their school days to make meaningful informed choices which encouraged them to 'take responsibility'. I helped children to consider what they could have done differently and what other outcomes were likely to occur as a consequence of different behaviours. We discussed how they could use more positive body language which was less defensive and hostile. We role-played an incident when they had been involved in conflict and how they could have handled it differently. I discussed with pupils how they could improve their response to conflict and avoid being involved in aggressive confrontations. This helped pupils who were frequently in trouble for bullying to develop more positive relationships with pupils and teachers.

The mentoring in groups meant that peer pressure could be openly discussed with pupils and the perceived gains and negative effects of conforming to it were highlighted. We discussed matters such as other pupils who had behaved like them previously who had left school and what they were doing now they had left school; pressure from peers to misbehave; and how they could achieve approval and positive interactions from pupils and teachers through more respectful behaviours rather than bullying.

I developed individualized weekly plans with mentees. They decided on what targets they wanted to set themselves each week to improve their behaviour, for example, not being sent out of class or given detention, not being involved in aggressive confrontations with teachers, and speaking to teachers and pupils more respectfully. We reviewed, on a weekly basis, the extent to which they had achieved their targets and what issues had negatively influenced their responses, and considered how these issues could be resolved. Our discussion and role-plays about how to respond to others more respectfully helped equip children with the autonomy and reflection to consider a range of responses and consider the consequences of their responses to conflict.

Youssef

Youssef was a pupil in Year 9 who I mentored once a week for a half-term; I spent about two hours with him each time I saw him. He was persistently in trouble with his teachers for bullying other children. Youssef was responding aggressively and abusively to teachers when they reprimanded him and often shouted and swore at them.

Youssef was frequently being excluded from school for beating children up and he was taken out of isolation to meet with me. He seemed both defensive and inquisitive when we first met. He sat with his feet up on the chairs, was constantly moving around and sat with his legs wide open. He expressed his frustrations about being put in isolation because he felt incredibly bored and angry as a consequence. His most significant grievance concerned the punishment and conflict he was constantly experiencing from his teachers and he felt that he was getting into trouble all the time and being 'picked on'. However, Youssef explained his reluctance to improve his behaviour because he felt it earned him lots of 'mates' and respect. He was reluctant to be obedient and compliant towards teachers because he was frightened of losing his 'mates' and their 'respect'.

I was concerned that Youssef might not want to improve his behaviour and might feel judged and defensive if I tried to help him change. However, he told me that he had just been given a week of detentions after school so he would probably not come to school for a week until the detentions had finished, although he was worried that if he did miss school he might have even more detentions to come back to. I sensed that Youssef felt helpless and entrapped within the punishment cycle he was experiencing. He didn't seem to know exactly how to adjust his behaviour to stop the punishment he was constantly experiencing or how to improve his relationships with his teachers. I told him that I noticed that being in trouble with teachers all the time was bothering him and asked him if he wanted me to help him address this issue; he told me that he did. This meant that he gave me permission to help him. By supporting Youssef to deal with the conflict with his teachers I could consequently help improve his behaviour and reduce his bullying.

One of the first things I wanted to do was help Youssef communicate more effectively with me. When I first met Youssef, he would not look me in the eye. I hoped that by encouraging him to look me in the eye more it would help him notice and understand my emotions and potentially develop his empathy. When Youssef had been arguing with one of his teachers, I asked him to role-play what had happened. Youssef demonstrated what had happened through role-play and I took the part of his teacher. After our role-play I asked Youssef why he thought his teacher responded the way he did and what alternative responses he could have provided. We discussed how I would respond to his behaviour if I was his teacher. This helped Youssef understand his teachers' perspectives and the challenges they have, which developed his 'empathetic understanding' and helped him make informed choices about his response.

Youssef had not previously been provided with consistent, structured and regular support to reflect on his behaviour. Nor had he been taught how to respond more respectfully. Although his teacher had sometimes spoken with Youssef about his problematic behaviour, this support was inconsistent and they were experiencing lots of conflict with one another which meant their relationship had deteriorated and become strained. However, Mr Baker was keen for me to work with Youssef and spent quite a lot of time discussing his behaviour with me. On one occasion, Youssef asked me to arrange to speak to his teacher so Youssef could apologize to him for his animosity towards him whilst I was present. I provided mediation with Youssef and his teacher so Youssef could express and articulate his feelings and listen to his teacher express his thoughts and feelings. As an 'outsider' I had not been involved in any of the conflict with them and helped improve their relationship by supporting them to understand one another's perspectives of each other and improve their communication with each other.

Youssef and I developed a trusting relationship as he confided in me, asked to see me, waited for me and even spent some of his break-times working on improving his behaviour with me. Youssef's relationships with his teachers and other pupils improved dramatically as he learnt to understand their perspectives in ways he hadn't done previously. He became more reflective and skilled in carefully considering his choices rather than just retaliating aggressively to conflict. He informed me that he had not realized how much he was hurting the pupils he was bullying, and the teachers he was being aggressive towards. Youssef stopped getting in trouble for bullying other pupils and became more respectful towards his teachers over the time that I worked with him.

Mark

A key question which needs asking before implementing a mentoring programme is: do children want to change or admit they have a problem? One child, Mark (Year 11), for whom I provided mentoring for about three sessions, felt that his behaviour was amusing and perceived it positively. When I challenged his behaviour by explaining how it was causing distress to other children and teachers he refused to work with me. As it became apparent that he did not want to improve his behaviour I concentrated my efforts on the children who felt frustrated with the consequences of their behaviour and who wanted to improve.

Group mentoring of Year 10 pupils

I occasionally mentored pupils in groups, but this was inconsistent and happened only a few times, as it depended on when Mr Hyde, head of Year 10, agreed to it. These children included Chloe, Ava, Vanessa and Megan. They told me that some children in another local school had been calling Ava names and threatening her so they were planning to have a fight with them after school to stick up for their 'mate', and Chloe said she had to stick up for Ava because she was her cousin. Chloe told me that her dad had taught her that she needed to 'stick up' for herself otherwise she would get bullied. I discussed with children why they were going to fight the other children and what the consequences of this behaviour might be. Throughout this process I started to understand why they were responding aggressively and how their personal backgrounds and peer pressure contributed to their response.

I helped convince them of the negative consequences which were likely to occur from their behaviour and we discussed and role-played strategies of how they could deal more respectfully with the conflict. I reminded them of the responsible role they were holding through the anti-bullying campaign they were leading. I told them that it would be unacceptable for them to campaign against bullying whilst also fighting with other children. They said they were grateful for the chance to help bullied pupils so they would not suffer like they had done. They did not have 'the fight', dealt with their issues through talking about them with the people they were supposed to be fighting with and thanked me for my input.

Reflections

Support for schools

If schools want to provide mentoring of pupils internally they can allocate weekly appointments for a member of the pastoral team to design and deliver the programme. External or internal provision to design and implement a pupil-led anti-bullying campaign is likely to be a success if children are actively involved in advocating for an anti-bullying culture. It would be particularly helpful if your school could employ an allocated member of staff to deal entirely with issues of bullying, particularly between pupils, and pupils and staff. Recommendations can also be made from a pupil-led campaign which can improve school practices for dealing with bullying.

External expertise to resolve school bullying can expand upon pastoral care provision and be a proactive approach to improving children's behaviour. It can be provided by researchers and charitable organizations. Some of these services could provide interventions which focus on supporting schools to develop their own resources to tackle bullying. Experts in the field of bullying can provide consultancy to senior managers who subsequently train all staff in tackling bullying and implementing pupil-led approaches.

Schools where staff feel they do not have the time to implement a mentoring programme for children who bully, or who cannot afford to pay for an external consultant, can draw upon community support to develop this programme. They could arrange for adults in their local community to be trained to provide mentoring for pupils. By expanding the individuals and organizations schools work with, many of whom are likely to be local to the school's community, they can have more resources to develop healthier relationships in school, so pupils, and pupils and teachers, improve how they interact with each other. It can also enhance children's social skills and reduce the use of overt punishments which are often perceived by those who are subject to them as ineffective means of improving their behaviour.

Benefits and obstacles

The most significant positive impact in the anti-bullying campaign was in the level of commitment and transformation I witnessed from several children who were involved. The campaign gained momentum as the children took a leading role in steering it forwards. It gave children the opportunity to articulate their feelings and emotions, and achieve respect and admiration from peers and staff through their work. Several children showed great commitment, reflected upon how their own behaviour had caused harm to others and committed themselves to improving their own behaviour whilst also supporting those victimized.

The mentoring programme helped children to stop responding aggressively to their peers and teachers, reflect upon their behaviour and learn how to respond to their peers and teachers more respectfully. Children's relationships with their peers and teachers improved as they articulated their thoughts and feelings more effectively, and enhanced their understanding of the perspective of others. Mentoring might have had a more significant impact if I had worked with pupils when they were in primary school which could have helped prevent some of the negative behaviours which had already developed. The improvements made were primarily at the pupil level and would have been more effective if staff would have been more able to commit to them. However, it was encouraging to observe children's social adjustment improve as they developed healthier relationships with themselves, and their peers and teachers.

Further recommendations

The project could have been enhanced through more thorough record keeping of what was done, the response of pupils, issues that arose and progress made. After the project had been implemented Mrs Shelton said she would have liked to have had a record of meetings with children showing what was discussed but there were confidentiality issues around this. For this project to have achieved its full potential, more staff would need to be actively involved in it. If this happened, it could be used to help improve how schools understand and respond to bullying. This anti-bullying initiative can also provide schools with an additional layer of intervention. Schools could apply jointly with researchers and/or anti-bullying practitioners to fund projects such as these.

The three months I spent in school meant that there were limitations to the deep-rooted changes to pupils, school practitioners and the school ethos. It also meant that a thorough evaluation was not carried out. However, this project was starting to making positive changes in how children thought and behaved which highlights the potential it has for further development. It has also led to a more evidence-based pupil-led intervention in Carfield Primary Academy, which is discussed in Chapters 7 and 8. The pupil-led intervention which it led to gives significant attention to the pupils' voices where pupils have an even greater role in developing and implementing interventions to address their specific experiences of bullying. It also includes more involvement with school staff, and further reflections on their involvement.

Tips for School Practitioners
'Mentoring for "Bullies"'

- Schedule weekly meetings with children who are persistently in trouble for bullying over a specified time, for example two to three months, with a member of staff who can provide specialist support such as a senior learning mentor or head of pastoral care. This can ensure enough time and attention is dedicated to examining in depth what the issues are, and that the mentee develops strategies to address these issues.

- When meeting with children to discuss their bullying, discuss why they behaved the way they did, how other people felt as a consequence and explore with them how they can behave more respectfully.

- Support children to help them make informed decisions about their behaviour; consider the different ways they respond to conflict and the likely outcomes of these responses. Reflect with children on what responses are most likely to be effective in resolving their problems.

- Children can experiment with different ways of behaving and likely outcomes through discussions, reflection and role-play.

- If children are reluctant to improve their behaviour because it helps them gain peer approval, focus on helping them improve aspects of behaviour which are causing them distress, such as getting into trouble with teachers, to realize how they will benefit from mentoring. It is important to get permission from children that they want to change.

Pupil-led anti-bullying campaigns

- Ask for pupil volunteers to lead the campaign who may have engaged in bullying previously but who are trying to improve their behaviour.

- Encourage children to be involved in deciding what work they will do, and how they will implement and present it.

- Help enhance children's communication skills and confidence through teaching them how to present their work effectively.

- Mentor the anti-bullying campaigners to deal adequately with their own experiences, and reactions to bullying.

- Facilitate 'Bullying: have your say' forums for pupils; this will help you listen to their specific experiences of bullying and can improve how staff and pupils respond to bullying.

Chapter 7

A Pupil-Led Anti-Bullying Intervention – Design and Implementation

Introduction

Outline

The pupil-led intervention in this chapter develops and expands on the anti-bullying initiative in the previous chapter. The intervention in this chapter was in Carfield Primary Academy (CPA). An evidence-based approach is provided where pupils are actively involved in designing, implementing and evaluating an anti-bullying intervention. Staff were also consulted with throughout the intervention. It consists of pupils working together to resolve their specific problems with bullying and expands on the 'Mentoring for "Bullies"' programme. This chapter focuses on how the intervention was designed and implemented and the following chapter outlines how it was evaluated by pupils and staff.

Purpose

The aim of this pupil-led intervention is to support children to have a leading role in understanding their experiences of bullying and develop strategies to address these issues. Previous chapters have demonstrated that most children are unsatisfied with their school's efforts to tackle bullying. Strategies used by schools to raise awareness of bullying often consist of passive and abstract anti-bullying messages such as anti-bullying posters which most pupils do not particularly care about. As Aalia (Year 5) explains, 'Most of the time all the posters are just on the floor and people don't even pick them up, they just walk all over them.' Children also felt that staff spoke about the problem of bullying and cyberbullying but not how to handle it. Taaliq (Year 5) explains, 'In assemblies they talk about stuff like anti-bullying and stuff on PCs but she doesn't actually talk about what they could do to stop the situation.'

Approaches which focus on teaching children about the problem of bullying without encouraging their participation, or learning what they can do to improve the issue, are often ineffective in changing the way children behave and respond to bullying. Taaliq feels a lot of children are disengaged from anti-bullying assemblies provided by teachers:

> The teacher does this assembly about bullying, the people who are getting bullied they're the only people who are looking to it. They look away, start chatting on a mat...we've had lots of assemblies and all of them just look back to see and then some of them are messing around, talking and getting moved.
>
> (Taaliq, Year 5, CPA)

Taaliq suggests that some pupils are bored, misbehave and get into trouble whilst they are being taught about bullying. This highlights the extent to which children feel their lessons about bullying are not relevant or helpful for them. Children in this book have demonstrated that schools should pay more attention to children's experiences and perspectives of bullying, and support them to have an input into how it is dealt with. This is likely to be more effective than adult-centred approaches where children who are taught about bullying can feel isolated from the issues which are supposed to be about them. The intervention in Hollybrook Academy has shown how pupils taking a central role in campaigning for their school's anti-bullying culture can be extremely effective. Such an approach involves children working in solidarity to help resolve their problems with bullying and improving their own responses.

Details of Research
Methods
This study used action research which involved collaborating with pupils and school practitioners to implement change through a pupil-led approach. Children are constructed as co-generators of new knowledge who disseminate their knowledge to, and with, researchers (Spears and Kofoed 2013). The process of action research involves planning a change; implementing a change; learning what happens following the

change; and planning further action (Kemmis and Wilkinson 1998). Pupils were actively involved in all stages of the research process. Staff were involved in planning and evaluating the intervention but did not seem to want to be involved in implementing it.

Qualitative approaches were used: focus groups, observations, individual interviews and children's diaries. Observational data was generated through field notes. Observations were used to record morning playtimes on a weekly basis for seven weeks. These observations focused on how a boy I mentored, Amir, interacted with other children and staff. Observation notes were also taken to document the implementation of intervention. They primarily focused on what we did in the intervention, how children and staff were responding to the intervention, and what issues were discussed. Notes were taken after each day I visited school to reflect on my experience, record my thoughts and feelings, and reflect on how the intervention could be developed. Twenty-three visits in total were made to Carfield Primary School. These visits involved meetings with staff and pupils to introduce the research, interviews with staff and students, implementing the intervention, evaluating the intervention and feeding back to the school what had been learnt and achieved.

All five children who participated in the anti-bullying group sessions were provided with a diary at the start of the intervention and asked to write in it regularly, document their interactions with other pupils and school staff, and reflect on their feelings. Children were also asked to note any incidents at school with other children which had caused them distress. I informed children they could return their diaries to me at the end of the intervention.

Participants and data collection
Recruitment
Participants were recruited from an inner-city primary school where the majority of pupils were from minority ethnic backgrounds. More than half of the pupils in the school were of Pakistani heritage. All children in this study were of Pakistani heritage apart from one pupil, Aalia, who was Indian.

The headteacher Mrs Griffiths gave consent for the study to be conducted in school as long as Mrs Adam (senior learning mentor) agreed to be the main point of contact and co-ordinate the project. Once Mrs Adam gave her consent, parents/guardians and pupils were required to provide their consent.

To begin the research, I introduced myself and outlined the project to the pupils in each of the two Year 5 classes (classes 5a and 5b). I informed children that they would be required to participate in focus group interviews and meet regularly to work together to design, implement and evaluate an anti-bullying intervention. Although Mrs Kahn told the children I spoke to in class 5a that they could not stop doing the work after a couple of weeks as she expected they would want to, I explained to children that they could withdraw from the study whenever they wanted to.

Details of students

Out of the 60 children who were given consent forms for their parents/guardians to sign, only five forms were returned with their signatures. These children formed the anti-bullying group. There were four females: Lily, Sunita, Yana and Aalia, and one male: Taaliq. All of these children were in class 5b and only one parent (Lily's mother) volunteered to be involved in the study. Mrs Kahn said that the low parental consent rate was probably because most of the parents could not understand English sufficiently to read the consent forms.

Children were interviewed when they were in Year 5 and Year 6 which meant that ages of participants ranged from 9 to 11. The mentoring involved supporting one boy, Amir, who was also in class 5b, who was persistently in trouble for bullying other children; staff were also concerned that he was also being bullied and ostracized. Amir's parents gave consent after they spoke with the new headteacher, Mrs Stephenson, about how the mentoring provision could help support him to improve his behaviour, as the school had started to exclude him for part of the school day. Amir was not involved in the design of the intervention but participated in the study throughout the implementation and evaluation phase.

Each of the five children who participated in the anti-bullying group were interviewed individually about their personal experiences of bullying, as a group interview would not have ensured sufficient confidentiality or depth for children to open up about their personal experiences. These pupils were subsequently interviewed in three focus groups. The first focus group was about designing an intervention and the second focus group honed in on children's ideas to clarify and refine them so an effective intervention could be developed. In the third focus group with children they evaluated the intervention. The child who was mentored, Amir, was interviewed individually after the mentoring and not in the group because of the personal nature of the work and the conflict between him and several children in the group. Table 7.1 demonstrates the forms of interviews with pupils in class 5b.

Table 7.1: Types of interviews with pupils in class 5b

Experiences	Designing an intervention	Evaluation
Individual interviews with anti-bullying group	Two focus groups with anti-bullying group	One focus group with anti-bullying group
		1 individual interview with mentee (Amir)

All interviews in this study with pupils and staff were semi-structured to provide both consistency in areas covered and freedom in attention to topics (O'Kane 2000). Focus groups encourage participants to talk with one another about the questions asked which can encourage more natural conversations than individual interviews (Duncan 1999). Repeated focus groups are referred to as sequential focus groups. Sequential focus groups are a good way to obtain pupils' views and feedback and find out where there is consensus. They also enable knowledge sharing, build collective narratives and allow for repeated sharing of knowledge which is deeper than if participants had only met once (Pritchard, Potter and Sauccucci 2009).

Details of staff

Staff who were interviewed in the focus group about children's experiences and designing the intervention consisted of four support staff. Although class teachers were invited to the meeting Mrs Adam informed me that they were too busy to attend. Details of the staff who participated in the interviews to design and evaluate the intervention (and their job titles) are provided in Table 7.2.

Table 7.2: Staff interviewed about the pupil-led intervention

Pupils' experiences and designing an intervention	Evaluation
Mrs Adam (senior learning mentor) Mrs Kahn (learning mentor) Mrs Nowak (learning support teacher) Mrs Iqbal (Year 3 teaching assistant)	Mrs Adam (senior learning mentor) Mrs Kahn (learning mentor)

Note: All the staff in the interviews were female.

Details of Intervention

The timespan of the design, implementation and evaluation of this study with pupils and staff was between May and June, and September to November. Between May and June children and staff were interviewed about children's experiences of school bullying. In September to November the intervention was implemented and evaluated by pupils and staff.

The following January I met with the school's behaviour manager to feed back what work we had done so she could develop it. I also provided training to staff about how to understand and respond to pupils' experiences of bullying. I explained what work I had done with pupils and staff, and how they could adapt it.

Interventions with the group of pupils and mentoring consisted of seven sessions which were provided on a weekly basis for 45 minutes to one hour. I also brought Amir and Taaliq together in a meeting in an additional session. Interventions were designed through session plans which included a title for each session and an outline of what would be covered.

Ethics

The project went through a rigorous ethical review prior to, during and after the study. Ethical approval was granted from Birmingham City University. I had described the study to children in classes 5a and 5b and answered their questions about it to ensure children gave their informed consent. After this, only children who had a parent/ guardian sign a consent form, and had signed their own consent form, participated in the study. Five staff and the two headteachers in Carfield Primary Academy volunteered to be involved in this research and support it. The pupils' class teachers when they were in 5b and moved to 6b both agreed to allow children to participate in this study and support the research.

Participants were informed that their data would be treated confidentially and were informed of their requirement to maintain confidentiality in focus groups. They were debriefed and informed of their right to withdraw. Pseudonyms are used for participants (staff and students) and the school. The risk of potential harm was monitored and reflexively assessed prior to, during and after interviews.

Design of intervention
Interviews with children and staff to design an intervention

All interviews were audio recorded and transcribed. Interview questions about children's experiences with staff and students focused on finding out about children's experiences of bullying and cyberbullying, what participants think people (e.g. staff and pupils) do about bullying, and what should be done about bullying. Please see Appendix 7 for the schedule of interview questions for children about their experiences of bullying.

Interview questions about developing an intervention with staff and students focused on what would help stop bullying, what work we could do to help and reflections on these suggestions. In addition, these questions addressed how bullying could be taken more seriously in school, how children can manage their feelings when they are bullied, the consequences of how bullying is usually dealt with, tackling cyberbullying and how peer relationships can be improved. In the first focus group with staff they were interviewed about children's experiences of bullying and how to develop an intervention. Please see Appendix 8 for a schedule of interview questions for staff about children's experiences of bullying. In Appendix 9 there is an interview schedule for the first phase of interview questions for children about how to develop an intervention with them. Please see Appendix 10 for the second phase of the focus group about how to develop an intervention with children. This interview schedule was used to refine the responses of children in the first interview about interventions. In Appendix 11 there is a schedule of interview questions for staff about how to develop an intervention.

Findings from individual interviews with children were used to develop the topics to be covered in the focus groups with staff and students about interventions. A framework analysis was implemented to analyze the interview data. This involved identifying the themes which emerged from the interviews. The themes were categories which encapsulated the data. These themes were then placed into broader categories which encapsulated a wider range of data within a particular topic. These broader categories are the thematic headings.

The thematic headings which arose from the interviews with children in the individual interviews about children's experiences and ideas for the intervention were the following (examples of themes are given in brackets): feelings from being bullied (e.g. feeling upset); forms of bullying (e.g. being called 'fat'); nuances (e.g. being friends with pupils who bully you so they don't bully you more); nature of bullying (e.g. escalates); teachers' positioning (e.g. bullying is not a priority); punishments (e.g. playtime gets stopped); cyberbullying (e.g. through gaming); why do children bully? (e.g. jealousy); handling bullying (e.g. letting go of anger); school anti-bullying strategy (e.g. posters).

Thematic headings which arose from interviewing staff about both children's experiences of bullying and developing an intervention were the following (examples of themes are given in brackets): issues are not caused by us/school (e.g. bullying comes from home); people tell us if they are bullied (e.g. children tell parents who tell us); bullying is dealt with (e.g. school thoroughly investigates bullying); 'it's not really bullying' (e.g. friends fall out and then make friends again); cyberbullying (e.g. through WhatsApp); anti-bullying strategies which we have tried/you could try (e.g. teach children not to hold a grudge).

The thematic headings which arose from interviewing pupils and staff were used to develop recommendations for the intervention which were pupil focused, for example providing pupils with a diary for an emotional outlet; staff focused, for example facilitating a meeting for staff and pupils to learn about children's experiences of bullying and discuss what can be done about it; and school focused, for example embedding teaching and learning about bullying into the school day.

I met with Mrs Adam to discuss these recommendations and decide which ideas we would put into practice. Mrs Adam asked me to work with the group of students to examine how they could respond better to conflict and have a positive outlet for their emotions. To provide individually tailored support to help pupils stop bullying, Mrs Adam asked me to mentor a boy, Amir, who was regularly in trouble for bullying and also victimized by other pupils. I agreed with Mrs Adam that at the end of working with pupils they would produce an output to show what they had done such as an assembly that was designed and implemented by pupils. Staff and pupils in this study would also meet together to enhance their understanding of one another's perspectives. Pupils would also explain what they had learned to staff and discuss how their learning could be used to help other pupils and staff. Mrs Adam asked me to work primarily with children rather than supporting staff which meant that this study did not significantly improve staff attitudes in understanding and resolving bullying. See Appendix 12 for the session outline of the anti-bullying group intervention which was delivered.

Group Work Implementation
Focus from staff

When I asked staff if they wanted me to support the children and staff to tackle bullying, they focused entirely on how I could help the children rather than themselves:

> Interviewer: Is there anything that you think I might be able to do that would be particularly helpful for the children? Or any ways I could support you?
>
> Mrs Adam: I think, getting them to understand a bit more of what bullying is and the difference between friendship issues and bullying issues, what they are. Even though we tell them, and they might see posters up about it, but it's actually getting them to understand.
>
> Mrs Nowak: Sometimes, they fall out and then the next day, they're probably best friends again.
>
> (First focus group with staff, CPA)

The staff did not seem to particularly want to be involved in the intervention. They were quite dismissive of children's relational problems and trivialized them. Instead of highlighting important areas for me to focus on in relation to bullying they discussed how children fall out with their friends and then make up. They gave the impression that children do not understand what constitutes bullying and attribute too many of their relational problems to bullying. However, they indicate that staff have a good understanding of bullying. Staff seemed to want me to teach children that the interactions with their peers which may cause them distress are not bullying: an ironic request since I was there to help them understand and resolve bullying. Perhaps staff hoped that if I taught children they are not being bullied, they would have fewer of the children's relational problems to have to deal with.

Cyberbullying and face-to-face bullying

All of the children who were involved in the anti-bullying group, apart from Yana, felt that face-to-face bullying was more serious than cyberbullying. As Aalia explains:

> Bullying is bad in person and more important because you know who it is, you see them every day, they're maybe in the same year as you and obviously you associate with them but they're basically in your face every

day, you can't get away from it whereas on laptops or iPad or phones or whatever you can delete the app, delete the game or whatever.

(Aalia, Year 5, CPA)

All of the children wanted help to resolve the problems of bullying they had in school which were not online, rather than cyberbullying, as they felt it was harder to ignore. Bullying through traditional means which was offline and in school meant that children were forced into close proximity with their 'bullies' on a daily basis and they felt entrapped. The face-to-face contact of school bullying meant their maltreatment was tied closely to their peer networks and friendship groups:

Sunita: The problem is that they're friends with your friends, you have to play with your friends but...

Aalia: They're never gonna get away from bullying.

(First focus group, Year 5, CPA)

Findings indicate that being in close physical proximity and regular contact with a perpetrator might be more distressing than bullying by someone who is anonymous. However, Yana felt that cyberbullying was just as stressful as face-to-face bullying: 'You can't do anything about that, you can block them but they can comment on you. Sometimes reporting doesn't do anything.' Conversely, the rest of the children felt they had more control over cyberbullying and that they could avoid it. Interestingly, the children in this study said they had not experienced much cyberbullying which may have contributed to them being less concerned by it.

Although these children had not necessarily been bullied online, they felt it was important to be safe online: 'Obviously you need to be careful what you're getting yourself into when you're playing games online' (Aalia). Furthermore, children felt that the anonymity which might arise from cyberbullying can make it harder to resolve as perpetrators cannot be identified, and individuals who are blocked can still make contact. However, Taaliq indicates that children are usually bullied online by people they know which supports the view of Wolke *et al.* (2017) who state that cyberbullying is usually a continuation of school bullying by traditional means where children are bullied online by those who bully them in school:

Aalia: Online bullying is harder to solve because you don't know who the person is, because they do fake names and stuff like that. And when it's in school you can see the person, it's face to face. It's not like they've got a bag over their head that you can't see their face.

Taaliq: When you block them they make another account, and it is mainly people that you know that start bullying you because they know stuff about you.

(Second focus group, Year 6, CPA)

Children discussed the abusive behaviours that their friends had experienced online but didn't particularly focus on their own experiences:

Taaliq: I know of one case where they started swearing at the other, then it started turning into only one is speaking saying really bad stuff to him, and his parents found out. They took the actual device and they said to this person, 'Stop saying rude stuff', and then they unfriended him and blocked him.

Interviewer: Where did he do this?

Taaliq: It was on an Xbox.

(Taaliq, Year 5, CPA)

The children in this study felt that online bullying was mostly through gaming. They thought that, in some cases, adults can help stop cyberbullying. In the example which has just been discussed, Taaliq explained how the parents of the child being bullied helped it to stop, which began by removing the device he was being bullied on. Aalia felt the elders in the mosque could help stop cyberbullying and find out who the perpetrators are: 'The elders can trace who it is like older people can trace it and they can deal with it from that.' The intervention in this study focuses on face-to-face bullying, rather than online bullying, because children were much more concerned with face-to-face bullying and wanted help to deal with it.

Release from negative feelings

Every child I interviewed about their experiences of bullying had been bullied and experienced significant distress as a consequence. School bullying was of paramount importance to them all and they felt it should be taken more seriously. At the beginning of the intervention, all the children focused on the bullying they experienced and usually did not consider how they subjected other children to maltreatment.

However, the intervention aimed to encourage them to reflect upon their behaviour rather than just focusing upon the hurt they experienced.

Children wanted to let go of the negative feelings they held from being bullied. Taaliq suggested, 'Write down everything that's worrying you then get a string and put it on a balloon and let the balloon go.' Mrs Adam also asked me to teach children to let go of their grudges and resentment towards those who had upset them. It was hoped that this work would provide an outlet for children to release their negative feelings from bullying.

'Empathetic understanding' amongst pupils and staff

There were differences between what the children understood to be bullying and what staff felt was bullying. Children felt staff did not realize their experiences of maltreatment were actually bullying and did not take their bullying seriously. They felt dealing with bullying was not a priority for staff. Interestingly, Yana said that teachers prioritize administrative tasks over combating bullying. She assumed that teachers do not have the time to resolve bullying and that it is not their duty to deal with bullying:

> Taaliq: They [teachers] wouldn't take it as seriously as you think they would.
>
> Sunita: They wouldn't consider it bullying...
>
> Yana: They've got a lot of things to do in their job, they've got to print out sheets and things like that, they must not have time, they must not think it's important because they must not have time to solve problems.
>
> (First focus group, Year 5, CPA)

I asked children to show me how they report bullying. They showed me that they report a specific act which has upset them, such as when a child repeatedly kicks their chair in class, to their teacher whilst she is teaching and did not explain what bullying they had previously been subjected to by the child who they were reporting. We reflected on the teacher's perspective by considering why she did not respond to the child whilst she was teaching. The pupils said she was too busy teaching a large class of pupils. We discussed and role-played how children could report bullying more effectively, for example, speaking to the teacher after class, explaining what had happened; the series of negative interactions they had experienced prior to the event; how they felt; and talking about what could be done about the problematic behaviour and how it could most effectively be resolved. Children said they thought this would be helpful and that they would try it.

I also gave all the children in the anti-bullying group the school's anti-bullying policy which defined bullying and specified how it would be dealt with. None of the children had seen the policy before and were not even aware that there was one. They said that the recommendations from the policy were good but that the school did not follow them; for example, Taaliq said that when there is bullying the school do not try to 'establish the causes', they just make those involved miss their playtime.

Considering alternative responses

Children were encouraged to explain how they felt when they had been bullied. They experienced several negative emotions such as 'sad', 'mad' and 'shocked'. We role-played the children's experiences of bullying and how they could challenge those who were abusive to them – internally by changing how they think, and externally based on how they respond. Sunita explained how she was upset when, last year, a girl wrote a note and put it in her shoe which read, 'You are so ugly.' The other children said that Sunita had a lot of positive qualities; they felt she was attractive, friendly, helpful and she often made them feel better when they were upset. They did not want to Sunita to see herself as ugly and wanted her to realize that the individual who insulted her might be jealous of her.

I asked children to reflect on how they can interpret and react to hurtful interactions more productively, rather than becoming extremely angry or upset. Sunita role-played how she might respond in future with comments such as 'I am not ugly, I am beautiful' and 'How are you, are you OK?' She said she might also ask the person if she had done something to upset them. Because children wanted to know why they were bullied we talked in depth about the underlying issues which contributed to their peers engaging in bullying such as being envious because of a desired quality that their target has and problems at home.

Some of the children in this study such as Aalia and Taaliq told us that that they didn't like their skin colour which they had been criticized for and felt insecure about. Taaliq and Aalia said they were too dark and Yana said she was pale but the other children said they liked the colour of the other children's skin. We looked at one another's skin tones and talked about how we are all a slightly different colour from each other and the children took an interest in this. We reflected on how we can learn to accept ourselves and our individuality rather than perceiving ourselves negatively. Children challenged one another's negative thoughts and encouraged their peers to see themselves more positively. They also reflected on the harm they had subjected their peers to. Sunita, who was upset when she was called 'ugly' had also called someone 'ugly' and Yana said she had spread rumours about another child which weren't true. This led to a discussion about why they engaged in bullying and they talked about how they might have felt angry or wanted to 'show off' and impress their friends. We talked about how children could stop engaging in bullying, respond more calmly and respectfully to those who bully and upset them and not take their anger out on others.

Problems with Amir

In our group discussions we talked about how popularity can contribute to bullying where, once a child has a problem with someone who is popular, those who 'follow' the popular person will all support them which contributes to a large group of pupils bullying another individual. This issue was particularly pertinent in the case of Amir, who was persistently targeted by a large group of Taaliq's friends. However, all of the children in the anti-bullying group, apart from Lily, said they have problems with Amir's behaviour and felt bullied by him. Amir often hit them, kicked them, swore at them and tormented them. Taaliq was particularly distressed by Amir's behaviour:

> Taaliq: You can call it bullying but you cannot really, because it is something that keeps on happening over and over again, then I would call it bullying. It's with one child [Amir] individually, just him.
>
> Interviewer: What does he keep doing all the time?
>
> Taaliq: Name calling, starting fights, starting trouble, anything like that. He used to do it with anyone he can find...but I take it more personally... I've spoken to teachers, my parents, his parents, but he just doesn't stop... You try and speak to him and he'll just swear at you. I think, personally, it's because he's jealous because...I'm not trying to say I'm better than him, but I am cleverer than him, and he tries to distract me from my work.
>
> (Taaliq, Year 5, CPA)

However, the staff who I interviewed felt that pupils target and ostracize Amir because he behaves socially inappropriately and has learning difficulties:

Mrs Kahn: I don't think bullying is the right label for some of the things that we get from the children, that are picked on in different ways. We've got Amir here, in Year 5, who is singled out because he annoys people.

Mrs Adam: But you could say that's bullying, in the sense that…

Mrs Kahn: But they wouldn't see it like that. They just don't want to be around a child who, to them, picks his nose all day long…he's got some kind of learning difficulty…

Interviewer: What kind of support would you like to deal with these issues? Or what could I do that would help you?

Mrs Iqbal: It's about informing our children about including children like Amir; to be more respectful about tolerance.

(First focus group with staff, CPA)

Although the staff asked me to teach children to include and accept Amir more, they did not ask for me to support them to improve their understanding and skills to resolve the bullying. I hoped that they might have done since they knew he was persistently having problems getting along with his peers and they had not been successful in helping to stop it.

The case with Amir was particularly complex because, on one hand, he was bullied by a large group of other children; on the other hand, most of the children felt victimized by him. I talked with the children regularly and in depth about Amir's behaviour, why he behaved the way he did, how it affected them and how they could help him. Yana and Aalia said they felt sorry for Amir because he had 'no friends'. We considered events through Amir's perspective and tried to understand why he is aggressive. They enthusiastically challenged each other's behaviour and came up with alternative ways of thinking and behaving that would be more productive and helpful. We used an example where Sunita had pushed Amir and kicked him when he swore at her. Aalia and Yana suggested that Sunita could pause for a few seconds to think about how to respond, then speak to Amir calmly and walk away from the situation if she is feeling angry. Sunita said she couldn't have just walked away because they were both in a queue but she could pause and respond more peacefully in future. Lily said these techniques were helping her to stop getting into fights and arguments.

To understand Amir's behaviour, children raised questions they would like to ask Amir and discussed explanations as to why he behaved that way; for example, Yana asked, 'Why do you kick and hurt people when they don't do anything to you?' They felt Amir might feel sad and angry, have problems at home, and want to speak to people and make friends but not know how to. They also felt that he might be motivated to bully others in order to get attention from his peers.

All the children felt that what Amir wanted most of all was to be accepted by Taaliq and the popular boys in his friendship group. They said that Amir wants to be just like Taaliq, and torments Taaliq because he is the most popular boy in their year. The children felt that if Taaliq was friends with Amir he would feel accepted and would stop being aggressive to people and upsetting everyone. Aalia said that because Taaliq is so popular, if he becomes friends with Amir and plays football with him then the other boys would follow. Taaliq explained that he would find this challenging because he has the most problems with Amir and gets particularly upset by his behaviour. However, Taaliq seemed to like the idea of being able to influence other children to follow him. He agreed to play with Amir and encourage his peers to include him as well. The other children in the group also agreed to be role-models to their peers by making more of an effort to speak with Amir and be pleasant towards him. However, when I saw the girls the following day they told me that Taaliq and Amir had been fighting and Taaliq had said he had already had enough of trying to help him.

One playtime I noticed that a boy was crying and trying to attack Amir, and Taaliq was physically holding the boy back. All the children seemed to be following Taaliq and running next to him. Sunita, Yana and Aalia said the boys crowd around Taaliq because he is so popular and they will do anything he asks. Progress was slow and just when I thought children were thinking differently they seemed to relapse into their usual behaviour. However, it was good to see Taaliq try to help resolve the conflict, particularly since he explained that he feels he has the most problems with Amir.

Mrs Kahn told me that Taaliq is not always there when Amir is being bullied; however, he causes the problems by manipulating the boys to bully Amir but rarely gets into trouble with teachers. The support staff said Taaliq is 'sly' and manipulates other children to bully Amir. They also told me that Taaliq had recently head-butted Amir.

However, despite relational problems with the children, as the work progressed Taaliq included Amir more in his friendship group and in football games at playtime. Children said that sometimes it was difficult to help Amir as when they had tried to help include him he swore at them and said things to upset them. However, over time the girls started to understand Amir's perspective more and, despite having difficulties, they started to include him more and defended him when he was victimized; this is discussed in more detail in the following chapter.

Mentoring with Amir

Introduction

I mentored Amir on a one-to-one basis. Mrs Adam explained that Amir is seen as a 'bully' because he can be aggressive and upsets other children but he also is bullied and has 'no friends' because she felt he didn't know how to interact with them. Amir has attention deficit hyperactivity disorder (ADHD) and received an official diagnosis and medication for his behaviour whilst I was working with him. Mrs Kahn explained that Amir can behave socially inappropriately, for example, by wiping his bogeys on other children. The headteacher said she was happy for me to take Amir out of his lesson to work with him because he is unlikely to pass his SATs exams.

Programme outline

In my first meeting with Amir I explained who I was and that I wanted to work with him to help him so he doesn't get into as much trouble and so he can get along better with people in school. I asked him if he wanted to work with me and he said he did. Mentoring was provided to help Amir and I understand why he engages in this behaviour, deal with the underlying issues which contribute to his aggressive behaviour and teach him how he can interact more respectfully with pupils and teachers.

Amir and I talked about incidents that had occurred throughout the week where there had been conflict between him and other pupils. Amir showed me how other children were mean to him and how he responded. When we discussed the arguments he had recently had with his peers we talked about what had happened, how he responded, likely consequences of his actions and how he could respond more respectfully next time. Through role-play we explored in a more concrete and illustrated way recent events, and potential consequences of his responses.

Observation of Amir's behaviour in the playground

From observing Amir in the playground, I realized that his behaviour was extremely disruptive to other pupils. He usually ensured he was the first person in the playground by running down the stairs where the other pupils were queueing and pushing them out of his way. In the playground I observed a large group of about ten children running away from Amir when he tapped them. When I watched Amir on the playground, I felt his desperation to be part of the popular group. It appeared that, sometimes, children were entertained by teasing and tormenting him and getting a reaction from him; for example, he ran after them when they ran away from him. Amir seemed to enjoy some of the attention from his peers and they appeared to enjoy tormenting him but then someone usually got upset and Amir was reprimanded by staff for his behaviour. Often, he became angry and upset when teachers reprimanded him for his behaviour and he started shouting and swearing at them. I noticed this vicious cycle in the playground frequently, particularly when I first started mentoring him.

On one occasion, Mrs Kahn told me Amir had kicked Yana in her private parts which had upset her, particularly since she was having her period. When I asked Amir about this, he asked me what child had told me and completely denied it. Amir explained to Mrs Kahn and I that the children upset him when they call him mean names when they see him. He told me he doesn't like the group I work with and asked me not to listen to them. He explained that children intentionally push him and tease him which makes him angry and he usually retaliates.

Core programme

Amir was particularly distressed by Taaliq who he said he doesn't get along with. He told me that Taaliq is mean to him and insults him by saying he is 'thick' and 'crap at football'. These comments hurt Amir and made him feel angry, particularly because he felt insecure about his academic ability. He also said he 'loved' playing football and was hoping to become a footballer when he grew up. We role-played these comments that Taaliq made about him, considered how he responded and discussed alternative ways of perceiving and responding more respectfully to comments such as these. Amir also showed me how his teachers responded when he misbehaved, for example, by contacting his parents, which helped me understand more clearly what had happened. Role-play provided a safe space for us to explore his behaviour, improve his communication skills and help break the pattern of his negative behaviour.

To improve Amir's communication, I asked him several times to pretend to be his idol Lionel Messi whilst I interviewed him. His communication suddenly improved as he spoke clearly and gave more eye contact. He improved his posture as he sat up straighter and was more confident, enthusiastic and animated in his communication. As I continued to work with Amir he started to speak more clearly and gave more eye contact throughout the entire mentoring sessions.

To help Amir realize the consequences of his behaviour we read an interview transcript of a child who I interviewed in a PRU named Carl. We reflected on how Carl's aggressive behaviour had led to him being permanently excluded from school. Amir took a great interest in this interview. I explained to Amir that if he continues to be aggressive to pupils and disruptive he is likely to get permanently excluded from school but if he improves his behaviour he will remain in school and get along better with his peers and teachers which can help improve his concentration and performance in his school work. I also reassured Amir that I would help him throughout this process. This resonated strongly with Amir and he informed me he was not being as aggressive to Taaliq and the other boys because he didn't want to 'end up like Carl'.

At the end of each session, Amir decided on his targets of how he wanted to behave throughout the week such as walking away from arguments, counting to five before he reacts and not swearing. In the following sessions, we reflected on the extent to which he had achieved his targets, what had contributed to him achieving or only partially achieving his targets and how he could improve his behaviour to more fully achieve his targets next time. Towards the end of the mentoring Amir told me he wasn't getting into trouble as much with his teachers or fighting with the other children. Amir's progress is documented more in the following chapter.

Issues

I was surprised when I observed Amir's behaviour in the playground as prior to this I did not realize the extent to which he was fighting with his peers on a daily basis. Sometimes I felt unsure as to whether there were enough concrete signs of Amir's behaviour improving when I observed him in the playground. He didn't always open up to me, and he said he was getting on well with other children when his teachers told me he was in trouble for fighting. I felt that sometimes he withheld information from me about how he was getting along with his peers. I even observed him being 'told off' by teachers but he told me he hadn't. I found it hard to work with Amir when he wasn't telling me the truth. I spoke to Amir about how important it was for him to be honest with me; I was aware that he was having problems with others and that is why I had come to help him. After I explained this to Amir a few times he started to be more honest and open. However, I became concerned about the amount of time I was investing in Amir when the progress with him appeared to be quite slow.

I often felt shut out by staff as they were reluctant to work with me from the beginning. Working in isolation limited the effectiveness of the intervention as the anti-bullying work seemed to be separate from the rest of school. It became clear that I would not be able to make significant improvements to how pupils and staff interacted with each other or the school's culture.

Bringing Amir and Taaliq together

Mrs Kahn and the children in the anti-bullying group suggested it would be beneficial for those who were in conflict with each other to have a meeting so they could speak about why they were not getting along, listen to each other and come up with strategies to resolve the problem. Taaliq said, 'I'd like it if the bully and the person sat in the same room and discussed what's the issue, then the person who's listening could think of a solution and maybe that could help it stop.'

Aalia suggested that children who are engaging in bullying should talk about how their emotions are contributing to their behaviour and explain why they are bullying. She also recommended that victimized children should explain their perspective to the person who is bullying them. She said, 'They should share their feelings of why they're bullying…by making the bully understand your point of view, maybe that would help.'

After I had worked individually with Amir and Taaliq I brought them together into a meeting to discuss why they were being mean towards each other and learn about one another's perspectives. Prior to the meeting, both Taaliq and Amir told me separately that they felt bullied by one another and were both distressed by this. However, Taaliq was seen by staff as engaging in bullying the most because he encouraged his friends to participate in bullying Amir. Even so, Amir often responded aggressively to Taaliq when he felt tormented by him.

I offered to provide mentoring for Taaliq on a one-to-one basis but staff did not allow this because he was performing well academically so they did not want me to take him out of his lessons. It might also have been because I was already working with him in the anti-bullying group sessions. Some of the other children in the anti-bullying group such as Yana and Aalia also wanted to have a meeting with Amir. However, involving other children could have led to Amir feeling more victimized. Consequently, the meeting just involved Taaliq and Amir as they had the most problems with one another.

Prior to bringing Taaliq and Amir together into a meeting, I checked with both of them that they were happy to sit with one another and that they would talk respectfully about their differences. I also supported them individually to prepare by considering what issues they wanted to address and how they could articulate their concerns productively. In my previous work with Amir and Taaliq I had helped them improve their skills in dealing with conflict more peacefully which also helped prepare them for their meeting together.

I started the meeting by explaining that they were there to talk about how they were getting along, their disagreements, why they behaved the way they did, how it made them feel and how they were going to get along with each other in future. They both talked about how they responded aggressively when the other said or did something mean to them. Taaliq looked visibly distressed when he discussed the problems he was having with Amir. He looked like he was going to cry when he realized that they were both moving into the same secondary school the following year. This realization highlighted the importance of working hard to resolve conflict between pupils who may be in quite close proximity for several years.

Taaliq discussed his past grievances with Amir. He explained how he felt hurt when Amir scratched him on the back with a sharp pencil when they were in reception class. Amir said he could not remember scratching Taaliq and apologized if he might have upset him. There had clearly been problems which had started over five years ago which Taaliq continued to feel hurt about. Amir explained that he was taking medication to improve his behavioural problems. Taaliq said he did not know this and felt it explained his behaviour but it wasn't a good enough reason to justify his behaviour. Taaliq said he thought it was best for them not to speak to each other so they could avoid fighting with one another. He asked Amir, 'What do you want from me?' to which Amir replied, 'Your friends.' Taaliq told Amir that his friends don't want to play with him because he kicks them and swears at them. However, Amir insisted that all he wants is to be friends with Taaliq's friends.

When Taaliq realized Amir's strong desire to be part of his friendship group he told Amir he would include him more in social activities such as football and encourage his friends to do so. However, Taaliq asked him to not kick them and swear at them, to which Amir agreed. Taaliq and Amir were both open about their feelings and what they wanted to achieve from the meeting. This helped clarify how they could move forwards in ways that would be beneficial to both of them as they developed 'empathetic understanding' of one another's perspective. After the meeting Taaliq felt sympathetic towards Amir because of his personal problems and difficulties interacting with his peers. The meeting with Amir and Taaliq was successful as they both listened to each other in depth, confided in one another and agreed how they would behave more respectfully with one another in future.

Meeting with Pupils and Learning Mentors

When I asked Mrs Adam if the children in the anti-bullying group could share what they had learnt in an assembly she said that there wasn't time but that they could meet with her and tell her what they had learnt. On the day I arrived to meet with Mrs Adam and the children, Mrs Adam told me that Mrs Kahn would also be in our meeting with the children. I hoped that this meeting would help pupils and staff understand the perspectives of one another and that pupils would show staff what they had learnt. This could improve how they understand and respond to bullying.

Unfortunately, the children were not happy about Mrs Kahn being present as they said she wouldn't listen to them and they didn't like her. However, Aalia and Yana said it was a chance to show them what they had learnt and the other children felt that, on balance, it was better to meet with Mrs Kahn and Mrs Adam and see if they would be listened to and taken seriously.

At the beginning of their meeting, Mrs Adam and Mrs Kahn asked the children what they had learnt. Mrs Kahn then asked them if they had thought about how Amir is bullied and what they can do to help. Yana said everyone is horrible to Amir, they fight with him, are rude to him, isolate him and call him names; it has become a daily routine. Mrs Kahn said standing back and not helping Amir is just as bad as bullying. However, Taaliq said that they get into trouble with teachers if they get involved or take sides.

Mrs Adam said to Yana and Aalia, 'You two are new so why did you get involved in the problems with Amir?' Yana and Aalia said they felt pressured by their peers to bully Amir. Mrs Kahn was quite confrontational with the children and abruptly said, 'You've had six weeks of tolerance; what have you learnt?' The children said they had learnt a lot about how to understand and help children who bully. Mrs Adam and Mrs Kahn did not seem to listen adequately to the children. Aalia said she tries to help Amir now and has learnt it is better to talk respectfully to people who are mean to her rather than get upset or angry. Sunita said that she thinks staff should support children and listen to them more. Mrs Kahn was defensive and replied, 'More; Sunita thinks we should do more; we take bullying very seriously.' At this point I explained that the children had been working really hard and wanted to share what they had learnt. Yana said, 'We've learned a lot and we've changed. We're not as rude and we help Amir; we are using our power to help rather than inflict pain.'

Children had written down things they wanted to say to Mrs Kahn and Mrs Adam but most of them did not say them as the learning mentors tended to focus on them bullying Amir. Lily had written down, 'Why can't teachers make time for children who get bullied?' but she didn't seem to dare say it. Yana said that she feels sorry for Amir who was forced to sit at the front of class by their class teacher, Mrs Bashir. The learning mentors said they would feed these recommendations back to Mrs Bashir and look into how he can be included more in class. Mrs Kahn told the children to ask the teacher to sit next to him. The children said they would ask their teacher.

In this case study, there were particular limitations to implementing a pupil-led approach when children were not adequately listened to or taken seriously by school staff. These children may be inadvertently learning, through observing how staff interact with pupils, how to undermine and humiliate individuals who are vulnerable.

Conclusion

A case study has been provided of how I implemented an evidence-based pupil-led intervention in Carfield Primary Academy. Approaches such as 'Mentoring for "Bullies"' discussed in earlier chapters have been expanded on in this chapter to include how to work with other pupils involved in the conflict.

How pupil-led approaches have been implemented in school with a small group of pupils has been discussed. Such approaches include strategies which support children to have an outlet for their negative feelings, learn more respectful ways of responding to bullying and enhance their understanding of the perspectives of those who don't fit in with their peers. The way staff relations with pupils restricted the voice of pupils has also been explained.

Chapter 8

A Pupil-Led Anti-Bullying Intervention – Evaluation

Introduction
Outline
This chapter examines how the pupils and staff evaluated the pupil-led intervention in Carfield Primary Academy after it had been implemented. The pupil-led intervention has been discussed in the previous chapter. To evaluate this intervention, Amir was interviewed individually, the pupils in the anti-bullying group were interviewed in a focus group, and Mrs Kahn and Mrs Adam (learning mentors) were interviewed together. Please see Appendix 13 for the interview questions which were used for pupils to evaluate the intervention and Appendix 14 for the interview questions which were used for staff to evaluate the intervention. Recommendations of ways you can develop this work and adapt it to the specific issues of bullying in your school are discussed.

Identifying themes in the data
To analyze the data, a framework analysis was used to identify the main themes arising from the data. This process involved identifying sub-themes, then themes, and finally thematic headings. The sub-themes were the categories which encapsulated the more specific details. These were placed into broader themes under thematic headings. Examples are provided throughout this chapter.

Amir's Evaluation of his Mentoring

Data analysis of Amir's interview

The thematic headings which emerged from interviewing Amir about his mentoring were 'improved relationships and behaviour' and 'perception of intervention'. The theme 'improved relationships and behaviour' focused on how Amir's relationships with his peers had improved because of the mentoring and how his negative behaviours and feelings had diminished. The 'perception of intervention' theme concerned how Amir felt positively about the mentoring, found it pleasant and wanted it to continue. It also includes how the mentoring can be developed, for example, through continued support.

Table 8.1 demonstrates the themes that emerged from Amir's evaluation of his mentoring.

Table 8.1: Themes of mentoring evaluation

Thematic heading	Themes and sub-themes		
Improved relationships and behaviour	Positive peer relationships (e.g. getting along with Taaliq now)	Staff relationships (e.g. rewarded by staff for good behaviour)	Negative behaviours and feelings have disappeared (e.g. stopped fighting)
Perception of intervention	Positive feelings (e.g. mentoring has been fun)	Continue and develop the mentoring (e.g. carry on mentoring me)	

Note: Sub-themes are in brackets.

Amir's perspective

I interviewed Amir straight after his last mentoring session. He felt the mentoring had a holistically positive impact on him:

> Interviewer: What do you think about the work we've done?
>
> Amir: I love it, but I still want you to teach me, because everything you done you help me. You help me on everything… I'm always going to remember you; I'm going to remember your name.
>
> (Amir, Year 6, CPA)

Amir felt he had been fully supported and guided in the mentoring which he felt had a life-changing positive impact on him. He appreciated and enjoyed the mentoring, and wanted it to continue throughout his last year in primary school and in secondary school; he commented that he wanted the mentoring 'until I leave…and I wish you could be in my next school'. When I asked Amir, 'What did you find useful that we've done?' he replied, 'Something fun. We got along with each other.' This highlights how Amir perceived the mentoring as pleasant and recreational. Amir appreciated the support he received and benefited from the mutually trusting relationship which developed. He confided in me and felt safe to learn and reflect on his behaviour. He explained how his aggressive behaviour towards Taaliq and other children had stopped:

> Last week when you taught us [Taaliq and me], that was the last time we had a fight. After that nothing happened with us two… All the stuff with the fights, all the naughty things I done I quitted it, it's all gone. Now I get on with the lesson… Taaliq don't annoy me and now we get along with each other. We stay with each other, we be nice to each other. We start being friends… I'm not bullied no more. I'm not that much bullying. They quitted… Taaliq and his friends said, 'Let's be friends.'
>
> (Amir, Year 6, CPA)

After Taaliq and Amir spoke about their problems with one another in their meeting, Amir said they were being more pleasant to one another, socializing and playing together. Since the meeting Amir said that he was no longer fighting with Taaliq or having problems with his peers and he was concentrating more on his school work. The headteacher, Mrs Stephenson, also told me that since I had worked with Amir and Taaliq together there had been no more reports of them having problems with each other whereas they used to frequently have fights and arguments with each other. Amir's relationships with staff had improved and he felt he was being rewarded more by teachers for his good behaviour; he explained that his teachers now 'add some minutes for extra playtime if we be good'.

Evaluation from the Anti-Bullying Group
Data analysis of the group work

Children in the anti-bullying group were interviewed straight after their last session to evaluate the intervention. However, my recorder only recorded the first five minutes of the interview, so I took notes of what I recalled from the interview. A week later I interviewed children again which meant that the longer-term changes, and relapses which might have occurred after the intervention had been implemented, might be evident.

The thematic headings which emerged were 'negative perceptions and interactions with teachers'; 'positive changes in self and others'; 'difficulties with changing'; and 'perceptions of intervention'. The thematic heading 'negative perceptions and interactions with teachers' was about how children felt towards the learning mentors (Mrs Adam and Mrs Kahn) after they had met with them to discuss what they had learnt from their anti-bullying work. It focused on how children perceived their relations with staff adversely. The theme 'positive changes in self and others' was about how children had improved their understanding of the perspectives of other pupils they were in conflict with and that they had improved their behaviour and had noticed changes in other children. It also included how there had been a reduction in negative behaviours towards others such as less fighting. The theme 'difficulties with changing' covered how pupils had not changed their behaviour and how staff did not encourage them to change, for example, telling them they had not improved. The 'perceptions of intervention' theme focused on how children perceived the intervention positively, and how they wanted it to develop.

Table 8.2 shows the themes which emerged from the children's evaluation of the intervention.

Table 8.2: Themes of pupil evaluation of group work

Thematic heading	Broad theme and sub-themes		
Negative perceptions and interactions with teachers	Teachers as unpleasant, dishonest and unhelpful (e.g. interrogated by staff)	Teachers didn't see our perspectives (staff sided with Amir)	Teachers don't listen to us (staff were not interested in what we had learned)
Positive changes in self and others	Understand the bully's perspective (e.g. they may have problems at home)	Improvements in self and others (e.g. learnt how to treat other pupils better)	Reduction in negative/aggressive behaviour (e.g. not had fights)
Difficulties with changing	Pupils haven't changed their behaviour (e.g. pupils who haven't worked on project won't listen to us)	Not encouraged by staff to improve (e.g. staff say we haven't changed)	
Perceptions of intervention	Work has been good and helpful (e.g. helped us loads)	Work should continue and develop (e.g. intervention should be in every school)	

Note: Sub-themes are in brackets.

Pupils' perspectives on the group work
Positive changes in pupils and reluctance of staff

Children felt the intervention had supported and guided them immensely; Aalia commented, 'You've helped us a lot, I can't even put it into words.' The children's learning had a far-reaching impact beyond just preventing bullying. Their understanding and compassion towards other children with whom they had been in conflict was inspiring, particularly towards Amir.

I've learned how to be more sympathetic towards others and understand how other people think. I've also learned how to control my anger and not use violence and to try and understand how being bad to him [Amir] affects his personal life and also affects his mind. We shouldn't make him feel left out... If you weren't here then I would not know Amir's part of the story, I wouldn't know how to be sympathetic towards Amir, I'd just follow the crowd and be really rude and nasty to Amir.

(Yana, Year 6, CPA)

In the quotation above, Yana explained how she had learnt to not be aggressive and instead interact more positively towards Amir. She understood how the bullying he was experiencing was negatively influencing how he thinks and feels. Yana reflected on how others had ostracized Amir and her newly developed 'empathetic understanding' towards him meant that she interacted with him more respectfully.

Children felt they had learnt to pay attention to people who were bullied and reflect upon their perspective: 'I've learned that it's not really nice to pick on Amir or anyone, and also to actually listen from what Amir's trying to say' (Sunita, Year 6). Aalia had learnt how to respond more peacefully to conflict: 'Recently we had a big fall out fight...normally I'd start screaming and shouting at them, "Why did you say these things to her?" But I've learned to be more calm.'

However, all the children were unhappy about the response from the learning mentors, Mrs Adam and Mrs Kahn, in our meeting with them. Aalia commented that she felt the learning mentors were investigating and scrutinizing them – 'It was like an interrogation' – and felt intimidated: 'They didn't listen to us like you do; I was scared!' Children suggested that staff were dishonest about how they handle bullying and covered up the problem as Yana, Taaliq and Aalia said, 'They're lying.' They thought the learning mentors blamed them for Amir being bullied and accused them of 'bullying Amir'.

Some children said that their teachers felt they had participated in an anti-bullying programme but had not improved: 'Our [class] teacher told us that, "you've been to a bullying club and you haven't done anything and nothing's changed"; and a lot has changed' (Sunita, Year 6). It appears that the learning mentors did not recognize or appreciate how children had developed throughout the intervention:

Sunita: We started talking about our personal bullying, but then they started saying, 'Oh, but what would happen if this happened to Amir?'

> Taaliq: They just kept on saying, 'You've been here for six weeks, what have you learnt?'
>
> Aalia: We had a lecture this morning about how everybody treats Amir. We're not saying that it's wrong to back up Amir...
>
> Interviewer: In retrospect, maybe I should have managed that meeting and talked more about what we'd learned, but I did try to say that.
>
> Aalia: I could see that you were trying to switch it.
>
> Sunita: Miss, I'm not being rude, but I just feel that they were talking over you.
>
> Yana: They probably were. They were acting as if she wasn't actually there.
>
> (Third focus group, Year 6, CPA)

Children felt that the staff did not particularly acknowledge my presence as they did not notice or listen to me. In the meeting with children and the learning mentors, it seemed that the mentors were as dismissive of me as they were of the children. Staff did not encourage children to improve their behaviour, nor did they show interest in what the children had learnt or try to understand their perspectives. Instead the mentors dismissed their views and experiences. Yet children felt they had made concrete efforts to help Amir but got into trouble with Mrs Bashir (their class teacher in Year 6) for getting involved:

> Aalia: When Amir had a fight with Umair most of the girls came in the room. And then Amir came in the room crying and everybody was laughing at him, and I stood up and I was defending him saying, 'Don't do that to him; just leave him alone.'
>
> Yana: I helped Amir today and then Miss just started shouting at me.
>
> (Third focus group, Year 6, CPA)

Self-development in self and others

Aalia said that she is no longer mean towards Amir, does not treat him as inferior any more and she has become more accepting of him:

> Aalia: I've seen changes in myself. I don't know about anyone else. Actually, I seen a change in Sunita.
>
> Interviewer: So how do you think you've changed, Aalia?
>
> Aalia: I don't speak to him in a horrible way. And I don't look at him like I used to before.

> Yana: I think we're more sympathetic, some more than others.
>
> Interviewer: And what about Sunita, how do you see a change in Sunita?
>
> Aalia: I can see since we've been doing this she speaks up a bit more.
>
> Yana: Yeah, she does actually.
>
> Aalia: She does, yeah. She's a bit braver.
>
> Sunita: I've seen a lot of changes in a bit of everyone now, they're actually getting together and being nice to him.
>
> (Third focus group, Year 6, CPA)

Children had noticed improvements in other pupils in the group; for example, Aalia noticed that Sunita expresses herself more, and had become more courageous. The children were more understanding and empathetic towards Amir and were being more pleasant towards him. However, Yana and Aalia felt Taaliq's behaviour towards Amir had not improved. Taaliq gave an ambiguous response about whether his behaviour had changed towards Amir after the intervention:

> Taaliq: It was good when I spoke with Amir, I understand him more and that he has problems. We've played together in the playground and not had any arguments since…
>
> Yana: He hasn't changed [about Taaliq].
>
> Aalia: He's really mean to Amir.
>
> Taaliq: I understand more about Amir when we had a meeting… He bullies for a reason. He annoys people or he kicks you or he does it for a reason.
>
> Interviewer: And do you think that's changed your behaviour?
>
> Yana: No.
>
> Taaliq: Kind of but not really.
>
> (Third focus group, Year 6, CPA)

Taaliq improved his understanding of Amir and learned why he upsets people. He said that they were getting along better but also that his behaviour had not significantly changed towards him. However, Amir felt Taaliq's behaviour had improved towards him as they had been playing football together and the fighting had stopped.

Sunita was concerned that once I stopped visiting the school, they might be pressured to revert back to their usual behaviour by other children who had not worked on the project because they could not influence them: 'I want you to come more because everyone, except for us, is just going to be "well, let's just carry on" because no one's going to listen to us, obviously.'

Aalia felt that what she had learnt would be useful and have a long-lasting impact, particularly when the children moved to secondary school and might feel more vulnerable, isolated and lonely:

> All of this we're probably going to use it when we come to secondary school... When we have no one to talk to we're going to be a bit more alone... All of this we've learned we should keep it in mind, take it to secondary school.
>
> (Aalia, Year 6, CPA)

Development of intervention

Children felt that those who had worked on our study were fortunate and that pupils such as Amir who had problems with his peers would particularly benefit from the work: 'I think other schools would benefit. Because in other schools, people like Amir are in the school then obviously, the next lucky six' (Aalia, Year 6).

Children wanted the sessions to be expanded; for example, Yana requested 'more sessions and for longer'. They also suggested that the project should continue with other pupils in schools: 'Stay here and work with different classes' (Yana). Taaliq felt that this project should be implemented in other schools where there is an individual who specializes in dealing with bullying: 'You can go into other schools as well and be known as the bullying woman.'

Evaluation of diaries

In the children's diaries the girls wrote about their personal experiences of bullying and the bullying they observed at school. However, Taaliq did not return his diary as he said he didn't want anyone to read it and share his inner thoughts.

Sunita wrote about how upset she felt when her friend kept running away from her. Her friend told her she hated her and hit her and then kept visiting her. Sunita commented, 'My friend keeps running away from me... I hate this, she is doing my head in she keeps coming to my house.' Sunita felt hurt and confused by her volatile relationship with her friend.

Lily wrote about a particularly personal experience of bullying she had at home whilst she was sitting in her front garden. Two girls swore at her, told her she was 'fat', laughed at her and said, 'You can't do nothing' and 'You're only little.' Lily wrote that she wanted help to take away her memories of her traumatic experience: 'Help me forget this awful day.' She also expressed how she felt upset about personal issues with her family situation when her dad got married to another woman. I hope that acknowledging and expressing her hurt feelings may have helped release some of her pain and sorrow. Lily reflected on what she had learned throughout our work together in her diary more than she did in the focus group. She also explained how she had started to discuss bullying with her family and learn more about how they can address it. These conversations with her family may help her improve how she responds to bullying in future:

> Now I know what I will do when there is a bullying situation. Since we have been talking about it, it has made me understand it more... I tell my family and I talk to them about what they think they could do and what they think bullying is all about.
>
> (Lily, diary, Year 6, CPA)

The diaries combined with the sessions helped children find a positive outlet for their emotions when they could not talk to their teachers:

> Yana: I loved the diary because it encouraged me to write things.
> Aalia: When you can't speak to the teacher about something then you can write it down.
>
> (Third focus group, Year 6, CPA)

Children felt that being heard and having their views paid attention to was particularly helpful for them; Aalia wrote in her diary: 'I really feel this book and the sessions with Elizabeth are helping us to get things off our chests because Elizabeth listens to what you have to say.' Yana wrote about how enjoyable she found the work we did in her diary and how she thinks it will help her address bullying from now on: 'I absolutely loved having fun with you and I've learned how to handle bullying and hope to use your advice in future.' Children enjoyed developing themselves, understanding their own experiences, and challenging their responses to conflict. Their appreciation of the project was partly because it directly involved them and the pupils and staff in their school. Children's engagement increased as they started to see improvements in how they responded to bullying and interacted with others. Their learning could be applied to deal with the bullying they were currently experiencing and help equip them to respond more effectively to other forms of bullying in the future.

Towards the end of her diary, Yana showed how she progressed from focusing on how Amir's behaviour upset her and her peers to recognizing the extent to which Amir had difficulties socializing with others; she started to empathize with him and understand that his being so alone contributed to his problematic behaviour:

> I feel that Amir doesn't know how to socialize with people…that's why he tries to get attention from people. Right now, it's 'wet play' and he's playing by himself while all the other boys, Leon, Taaliq etc. are playing together in a huge group.
>
> (Yana, diary, Year 6)

Evaluation from Mrs Kahn and Mrs Adam
Data analysis of interview with Mrs Kahn and Mrs Adam

To evaluate the intervention, Mrs Kahn and Mrs Adam (learning mentors) were the only staff who volunteered to be interviewed as Mrs Adam explained that the other staff were too busy. Two thematic headings emerged from their interview which were 'positive impact on pupils' and 'involvement of staff and school community'. The thematic heading 'positive impact on pupils' is about how pupils benefited from the project. Mrs Kahn and Mrs Adam felt that the pupils benefited from working with an external professional and that pupils improved their knowledge about bullying, particularly the girls. The thematic heading 'involvement of staff and school community' covers how staff perceived the pupil-led intervention in terms of the impact on themselves, colleagues, other pupils (who were not involved in the intervention) and parents. Staff also provided recommendations for how the work can be developed.

Table 8.3 shows the themes which emerged from the interview with Mrs Adam and Mrs Kahn when they evaluated the pupil-led intervention.

Table 8.3: Themes from staff evaluation

Thematic heading	Broad themes and sub-themes			
Positive impact on pupils	Working with an 'outsider' (e.g. good to have children talk to someone different)	Improved understanding and reflection (e.g. children realized they were wrong)	Have the children changed? (e.g. girls have changed)	
Involvement of staff and school community	We don't need to improve (e.g. just focus on pupils)	Work with staff (e.g. no changes in staff)	Work with other pupils and classes (e.g. with Years 1 and 2)	Parents (e.g. parents didn't want to be involved)

Note: Sub-themes are in brackets.

Mrs Adam's and Mrs Kahn's perspectives
Disengagement from staff

It has been discussed in the previous chapter how there had been very little engagement from staff as they seemed to be resistant towards the intervention. Mrs Kahn highlighted how the staff did not get involved in the project and most of them were not aware of it:

> Maybe if a TA [teaching assistant] had come on board with you, you were feeding back to the class TA; she'd be able to keep an eye on what you've been doing with the kids so she can see actually what have they been taught and what they are actually doing. Because it's very separate I don't think anybody really knows until today exactly what they've been asked to do.
>
> (Mrs Kahn, staff evaluation interview, CPA)

Mrs Kahn and her colleagues didn't know much about the pupil-led intervention until they had met with the children in the anti-bullying group at the end of the project. In her quotation she indicates that a teaching assistant might have been able to monitor this work and place it under supervision and scrutiny. Unfortunately, the staff were not aware of what the children were learning.

The children in the anti-bullying group felt that it was inappropriate that the learning mentors were so judgemental of their progress, particularly because they didn't have much contact with them and explained that they hardly saw Mrs Kahn:

Aalia: Miss Kahn was like 'Oh, I've been in your class since Year 5'. Before Year 5 was she in our class?

Sunita: She was never in our class.

Aalia: She only used to come in once a week for five or ten minutes.

(Third focus group, Year 6, CPA)

Progress with children

When Mrs Adam and Mrs Kahn spoke to the children in the meeting they realized how much they had learned:

> They came across as quite positive and a lot more understanding regarding bullying and, actually, being able to identify what they had done and what had been going on over the past year or so, it was good that they were reflecting and able to see that from a different point of view for a change.

(Mrs Adam, staff evaluation interview, CPA)

Mrs Adam felt that children had learnt more about bullying, thought about their own behaviour and enhanced their understanding of the perspectives of others. Mrs Kahn and Mrs Adam did not specifically comment on Amir's behaviour; this may have been because they did not discuss it with him and had not had much contact with him since they did not work in his class.

Mrs Kahn felt that the children realized that their behaviour in the past towards Amir was unacceptable. However, she wasn't sure if they could improve their behaviour and put their learning into practice. She implied that she had not yet witnessed them improve their behaviour:

> They knew what they were doing was wrong, and it would be good to see actually if they put that into practice. Because saying, 'We recognize what we're doing is wrong' but then actually putting it into practice and trying to stop it would be brilliant to see them do.

(Mrs Kahn, staff evaluation interview, CPA)

External support

Mrs Adam felt it was beneficial to have external support from someone who was not dealing with bullying on a day-to-day basis. She felt this external provision where children were supported to investigate the issues improved their understanding and helped them realize how important bullying is:

> Having somebody from outside coming to work with them is a bit more productive, because, for us, we're dealing with it every day, we're talking to them on a regular basis about the way they are to one another. I think as yourself, knowing that it's a research thing makes them look at something in a different way and maybe makes them realize how serious it is.
>
> (Mrs Adam, staff evaluation interview, CPA)

Drawing upon external expertise for support to deal with bullying would be beneficial, according to Mrs Adam, in particularly complex cases when all interventions staff have tried have been unsuccessful. Mrs Adam also indicates that children may respond more positively to external support: 'External help should be when it's really difficult, when you feel that whatever you've done in school hasn't helped…because it's somebody coming from outside and they respond differently.'

Barriers to progress

Mrs Adam and Mrs Kahn felt that the girls had responded positively but that Taaliq was more reserved and less involved: 'They seem to have responded quite well. I was wondering about Taaliq. He seemed very quiet; didn't seem to be as engaged as the girls were.' Mrs Kahn explains why she thinks Taaliq is more detached than the girls:

> Taaliq's quiet because you're going to go and he's going be left with us so I think he's very cautious about what he'll say. It'll be a case of how much he takes on board, will everything just fall back in the way it was before you were here or will they actually take on board what you've actually said?
>
> (Mrs Kahn, staff evaluation interview, CPA)

Mrs Kahn felt Taaliq was aware that I was leaving and that things would go back to how they were before. She implies that his caution and intelligence has contributed to him not articulating his voice. Children may suppress their voice in school as they learn that articulating their voice does not benefit them and can leave them vulnerable.

Mrs Kahn makes it perfectly clear that the staff are not going to reinforce what I have taught children. She indicates peer pressure and normalized practices in school are likely to encourage children to engage in bullying rather than challenge these norms and share what they have learnt: 'It'll make a tiny bit of impact, but the pressure of what the other children think they should do will probably bring them back to behaving that same way that they used to because there's only a few of them.'

Paradoxically, staff did not seem to have improved their understanding or behaviour:

> Interviewer: Do you think it's had an impact on school staff, this work, or do you think it's mainly involved working with the pupils?
>
> Mrs Adam: I think it's mainly involved working with the pupils.
>
> (Mrs Adam, staff evaluation interview, CPA)

However, Mrs Adam felt that the intervention helped her learn to encourage children to think more deeply: 'What we've learned is maybe sometimes asking them to reflect on their behaviour.' However, Mrs Adam felt that the learning mentors did not need to improve how they responded to bullying as they always did so effectively and she has ample time to speak to all the pupils involved:

> Whenever there's a bullying issue we [the mentors] will deal with it and we speak to all the children, not just the ones that are involved but any bystanders as well, we speak to the class as well, and we might do that individually, so we find out the whole bigger picture, we have the time to do that. But I think with teachers it's different, and with TAs [teaching assistants]. I think that question you need to put to them, because I could say, 'Yes, I think they need it', but then they might say, 'We haven't got the time' or 'We don't need it.'
>
> (Mrs Adam, staff evaluation interview, CPA)

Mrs Adam focuses on how she deals with bullying when it occurs rather than using any preventative methods. She perceives bullying as an isolated incident rather than considering how it is entrenched in everyday practices in school. Mrs Adam's view of her own effectiveness contrasts significantly with how the children felt staff responded to bullying, and how they perceived her as dismissive when they spoke to her about what they had learned. She indicates that the teaching assistants and teachers may need more support in dealing with bullying but they might not acknowledge this. She highlights a degree of defensiveness and an unwillingness in herself and, to some extent, the staff to acknowledge their own lack of understanding of bullying and how to address it.

Staff views on how the intervention can be developed

Mrs Kahn suggests it might be more effective to work with children who are showing early signs of behavioural problems to develop an intervention rather than allowing the problems to escalate: 'I think if we can target pupils that we know are now problematic in Year 1 and 2, if we can nip it in the bud now that might be more effective.' However, Mrs Adam does not consider the issues that children have in the early years of school as bullying as she asserts, 'It's not bullying issues in Year 1 and 2.'

Involving more parents could have helped make meaningful changes by meeting with them and informing them about the project: 'If we maybe made awareness for parents and let them know what to do if they had concerns as well' (Mrs Kahn). However, I arranged for letters to be sent out to all the parents in Year 5, informing them of the project and asking if they would like to be involved in the project. Mrs Kahn pointed out that parents' reluctance to be involved could have been due to many of them not understanding English because English may have been their second language: 'Maybe it's just that they haven't understood what it's about, because a lot of them maybe don't read or write in English.'

Feedback to School

After I had evaluated the intervention with pupils and learning mentors I met with the behaviour manager, Mrs Siddique, to inform her about the work I had done with the children and how she could continue it. Mrs Siddique told me that she did not know anything about it. However, she told me that since I had been at the school there had been a noticeable reduction in reports of bad behaviour through behavioural slips of the pupils in the anti-bullying group and the other pupils in their class. She asked me to continue doing the project with the children and liaise with the school council to show them what we had done. Mrs Siddique also suggested that the children in the anti-bullying group could become peer mentors. I informed her that Mrs Adam told me that the project with the children had to finish so they could concentrate on their SATs. I also explained that I wanted to work with the school practitioners so they could embed pupil-led approaches into their practice. Mrs Siddique said she did not have time to work on this project and asked Mrs Adam to lead on it. However, Mrs Adam told her that she was too busy, and that the school had had peer mentors before which the children just used as an excuse to talk about matters unrelated to bullying. She also said the children in the group were not the best children to work with and Aalia had 'friendship issues'.

At the end of the study I provided training to the staff about my research and pupil-led approaches. When I gave them the opportunity to ask me any questions, none of them did so. Furthermore, none of the learning mentors attended the session. After I had trained the staff the class teacher of the pupils in the project, Mrs Bashir, told me that all the girls had improved their behaviour and were helping Amir by including him more and 'sticking up for him'. She said they were writing letters to her about issues which affected them and when a pupil had been aggressive to another pupil, they wrote down what had happened and how they thought it should be dealt with. Mrs Bashir said Amir had started to pause and reflect rather than retaliate against children who tormented him. Although, she said that Taaliq was still secretive and manipulating the children in his class, the girls were realizing what Taaliq was doing and were not going along with this any more. I got the impression that Mrs Bashir was blaming Taaliq for all the problems and did not understand his perspective. She didn't seem particularly concerned about his behaviour and he rarely got punished by staff for it. When I had previously offered to work with Taaliq individually she did not agree to let me take him out of class because he was performing well academically, whereas the headteacher did with Amir because he was unlikely to pass any of his exams. However, bullying should not be separated from academic learning as it can have a negative impact, as Aalia explains, 'You have the person who's bullying you and your learning muddled up together, you can't do anything'.

I spoke with the headteacher and behaviour manager about how difficult it had been to get the staff involved in this work. The headteacher said the staff were not even co-operating with teaching and learning requirements but that they had to be involved in tackling bullying.

Researcher's Perspective

Reflections

The project had a successful outcome with the pupils involved and I could see how they had changed and developed, particularly towards the end of the project. Children progressed from focusing on the bullying they experienced to reflecting on their own behaviour and changing how they responded to conflict. This helped them interact more respectfully with their peers and resolve many of their issues of bullying. They felt more in control of managing their peer relations and had realized the negative impact of retaliating. Consequently, they significantly reduced their aggressive responses which prevented bullying from escalating.

In the first focus group I facilitated with staff they made it clear that did not want me to help them improve their knowledge or practice. They only wanted me to focus on the pupils. Interestingly, none of the teachers volunteered to be interviewed or were involved in the intervention. Ironically, the staff did not want to improve but expected the children to do so. I found it difficult working in isolation from staff when the project had been designed specifically to involve them. Often most of the staff did not even speak to me or acknowledge me when I was in school. However, a few members of staff asked me what I was doing when I was observing children in the playground and I spoke with a couple of SEN teachers about Amir and who were quite informative about him and his family background.

When I did my first playground observation when the children were in Year 5, Mrs Bashir (the children's class teacher in Year 6) asked me what I was doing. I explained that I was developing a pupil-led intervention on bullying and she walked away. In the evaluation interview with children they said they had noticed that the learning mentors were dismissive of me. At the end of the intervention when pupils met with Mrs Kahn and Mrs Adam, Mrs Kahn accused the children of not changing without finding out what they had learned and what they had done.

This project highlights that there were substantial issues with staff who were resistant to the intervention and did not pay enough attention to their pupils' voices. The issue of staff not listening to pupils needs to be adequately addressed in order to improve the school ethos and ensure that staff provide a good example to students on how to respond to bullying. French, Lowe and Nassem (2018) assert that pupil-led research requires repositioning pupils as active agents and reconceptualizing the traditional hierarchical relationships where teachers tend to dominate pupils. Although, most of the staff in this study were not prepared to sacrifice traditional hierarchies of power for the benefit of their pupils. However, this study has shown how, despite the reluctance of staff to engage in pupil-led approaches, pupils can still make significant progress and reposition themselves as active agents.

In many ways, children changed because the way they understood bullying, perceived their own behaviour and learnt about the perspectives of other pupils improved. They started to consider how to respond more peacefully to conflict in ways they hadn't done before. Although children felt their behaviour had changed there were some relapses. To overcome this, interventions should be carried out over quite a substantial period of time, perhaps two to three months, for meaningful changes to be made. Pupils need to be encouraged by their peers, staff and parents to improve their behaviour and when their behaviour does relapse, they should be encouraged to try again, be provided with guidance on how to change and supported to improve their understanding of bullying and behaviour.

This study demonstrates how children improved their understanding and response to bullying through open dialogue and reflection with me and with their peers. By talking about issues which directly affect them and working together to consider the various ways they can respond to bullying respectfully, children can learn how to productively exercise their agency and articulate their voice. These strategies helped equip children to deal with the challenges which can arise in relation to bullying and empower them throughout their lives.

Several children such as Yana and Amir enjoyed the project which helped maintain their interest. Children respectfully challenged one another's understanding and response to decide the most effective strategies to resolve their specific issues of bullying. Some of these children could become anti-bullying advisors who help address bullying in school and teach other children what they have learned. The approaches used in this intervention could have been used to improve practices in school for tackling bullying but, in this particular case, the school was not engaged enough for this. An intervention is likely to be more successful if it involves staff who want to develop, learn and change throughout the work as well as pupils.

Pupil-led approaches such as these provide an excellent opportunity for staff to harness pupil voice and develop interventions. However, as Yana points out, this requires 'teachers [to] take time out to listen to individual pupils'. Perhaps you can provide opportunities in some of your lessons to listen to pupils and understand their perspectives. In doing so, you will enhance your knowledge of bullying and strategies to resolve it.

Both Taaliq and Amir would have liked more sessions where I brought them together so bringing pupils who are in conflict with one another together for several meetings could be advantageous and may increase the likelihood of more long-term improvements. In addition, some children also wanted to meet with Amir so I could have invited more children to meet individually with those whom I mentor.

Meeting with staff at the beginning of the project to introduce myself and the intervention could have increased their engagement. However, I had planned to do this but the meeting had been cancelled by the previous headteacher. The headteacher who agreed for the school to participate in the project, Mrs Griffiths, had left and there had been several changes in staffing in the senior leadership team and school governance which might have shifted the focus of staff.

How schools can develop the initiative

Schools could have a member of staff such as a learning mentor to work with pupils and staff to implement pupil-led anti-bullying strategies to combat bullying. This could consist of working with a group of staff and pupils who volunteer to find out about pupils' experiences of bullying, how bullying is currently dealt with, and how it should be dealt with. From this dialogue, strategies could be implemented to deal with children's specific experiences of bullying. This process could also be used effectively to understand and tackle both bullying and cyberbullying. An advantage of a pupil-led approach to cyberbullying is that you will keep up to date with how children communicate online.

At the end of the intervention it is important for children to have an output to show and share with pupils and staff what they have learnt; for example, they could design and implement a pupil-led assembly or play. They could also write an information leaflet, anti-bullying policy or story, based on their experiences, to help educate their peers about bullying and what to do about it. Children could also meet with the school council, pupil and staff ABAG and/or staff to show what they have learnt and suggest strategies which can improve understanding of bullying and how it is dealt with. To share this knowledge, children involved in the intervention could support a member of staff to train other children and staff to design and implement a campaign to deal with their experiences of bullying. Through this process, pupil-led approaches become embedded in the school's culture.

Children can be provided with diaries and encouraged to write in them in class on a daily or weekly basis for the period of time that you are covering the topic of bullying, perhaps over about six weeks. Diaries can be stored in locked cabinets to ensure they are confidential. Alternatively, children could be provided with a diary to write in at home and you can read the diary at the end of the intervention. Ask children to write about their daily experiences of school and how they feel about them. They can include positive as well as negative experiences. Tell children that you can only look at them if they want you to so they can be confidential to the children if they want them to be. Emphasize to children that their diaries are not a list to report everything negative that people have done to them. Rather, diaries are an opportunity for them to reflect on what has happened to them and how they respond. You could also ask children who are bullied or who are being bullied to write in a diary so they have an emotional outlet. This can be used as a resource for you both to read and reflect on, and can enhance your understanding of their perspective.

Provide mentoring for children who persistently engage in bullying. Facilitate meetings between the mentor and the pupils they are having conflict with, ideally with just two pupils. Investigate with children the underlying reasons why children engage in bullying and use this knowledge to help pupils and staff to understand and resolve bullying. Ask children to consider alternative ways they could interpret upsetting comments others make about them and to reflect on how they can more effectively manage their emotions. Support them to internally and externally challenge their current thoughts and feelings and their response to their maltreatment. Show children how they can question the perpetrator's judgement of them. This will help children to construct themselves more positively and regain some power from individuals who are abusive towards them. Activities such as role-play with discussions and reflection can help children to analyze what has happened and reflect on their previous behaviour. Role-playing more respectful responses can help children develop their resources to respond more productively to conflict. Discussions about how to respond to bullying can help children consider a range of alternative responses and make a more informed decision about which strategies are the most effective. Staff involved in these conversations can also reflect upon their own responses to bullying and consider the most effective strategies to use in future.

Throughout this process critically consider how you and your colleagues respond to bullying rather than just placing all the responsibility on children. Discuss with colleagues how you can respond more effectively to pupils' unique and complex experiences of bullying, both individually and collectively. To enhance 'healthy relationships' between pupils and staff, meet with pupils at the end of the pupil-led anti-bullying intervention to find out what they have learnt and consider how, based on their feedback, you can work with colleagues to improve how bullying is understood and resolved between pupils, and between pupils and staff. Issues which may arise from pupil-led interventions to address maltreatment between pupils and staff could be incorporated into your school's anti-bullying policy or be used to develop an anti-bullying policy regarding bullying between staff and pupils. Furthermore, an external member of staff could work in schools to deal entirely with bullying, and develop interventions and recommendations which pay substantial attention to the voice of pupils and use this to improve how schools address bullying.

Conclusion

The pupil-led approaches discussed in this chapter and Chapter 7 have helped to reduce aggression in children, provided them with the skills to respond more calmly and thoughtfully to the different problems of bullying they experience, and have improved their relationships with children with whom they are in conflict. Consequently, bullying has been reduced and healthier relationships between pupils have been established. Approaches have been recommended which aim to improve what children learn about bullying and help them reflect upon how they respond to it. The difficulties children can experience when they are trying to improve their behaviour have been discussed, and ways you can support them throughout this process have been outlined. Strategies have also been recommended for how staff can improve their understanding and responses to bullying through engaging in pupil-led approaches. How staff and pupils have evaluated this project has been analyzed. Ideas about how this intervention can be developed and used to improve relationships between pupils and staff have also been outlined.

Chapter 9

Conclusion

Introduction

This chapter begins by explaining how *The Teacher's Guide to Resolving School Bullying* has addressed important aspects of bullying which other books have overlooked. It then draws together the key themes and strategies to help you understand and respond to children's complex experiences of school bullying.

The empirical research underpinning this book has been developed primarily from interviewing children about their experiences of bullying and how it should be resolved. In my experience, until now, the child's voice has not been substantially harnessed to help school practitioners understand the nature of bullying and how to address it. My approach contrasts with the over-reliance on statistics that dominate research on school bullying, which overlooks the child's voice and does not address the underlying reasons behind the bullying.

While traditional approaches focus primarily on understanding bullying between pupils, this book has examined bullying between pupils, bullying between pupils and teachers and bullying at the school level where systemic bullying is considered. A whole-school approach is recommended by the traditional model to tackle bullying but this has a rigid view of power imbalance which implies that there must be a clear power imbalance between individuals. Consequently, it does not pay enough attention to the nuances in power relations. It tends to overlook the complexity of the teachers' role in bullying, and how there can be power struggles between pupils and teachers. Neither does the traditional approach have sufficient understanding of systemic bullying and how to deal with it. However, *The Teacher's Guide to Resolving School Bullying* uses a holistic approach to consider the nuanced ways in which power operates; children's and teachers' subjective perspectives; and ambiguous cases so that you can deal with the forms of bullying which are commonplace in your school.

Key Themes and Anti-Bullying Strategies
Bullying as a spectrum

It is helpful to construct bullying as a spectrum of covert and/or overt aggression which ranges from mild to severe rather than defining bullying as a binary phenomenon whereby children are either clearly being bullied or they are not. Findings in this book have challenged the idea of bullying involving a clear imbalance of power by demonstrating how bullying can involve power struggles, for example, between pupils and teachers. Perceiving bullying as a spectrum rather than a binary phenomenon will help you support children even if bullying is mild, complex and 'grey' so that earlier and more effective interventions can be developed. Understanding bullying as a spectrum will reduce the likelihood of teachers dismissing children's experiences of maltreatment as 'not really bullying' and help resolve the conflict, tensions and distress which children are currently experiencing.

Consult with children to enhance your understanding of school bullying. Speak with children and find out about: their experiences of bullying; what is usually done about bullying; and what should be done about bullying. Share your findings with colleagues and collaborate with staff and pupils to bring about the most effective strategies to resolve children's complex experiences of bullying.

Functional bullying

Children who engaged in bullying were often popular and their bullying was often approved of by pupils and teachers. Meanwhile, children who were marginalized (usually working-class males who had learning difficulties) were often targeted by teachers and retaliated aggressively. They were perceived as 'bullies' and went through an ineffective cycle of punishments from teachers.

Work with other pupils and teachers to challenge normalized practices which enable bullying. Support them to understand the perspectives of those who are victimized, and encourage pupils to challenge peer group norms where certain children achieve status through ostracizing other pupils. One way to do this is to help those who are popular to gain status with peers by including pupils who are marginalized so they maintain social approval whilst also refraining from bullying.

A personalized approach to pupil-led approaches

Learning about bullying through abstract means such as plays about fictional characters may encourage children to reflect upon the negative consequences of bullying. However, it does not necessarily teach children how to improve their behaviour. The strategies discussed in this book focus directly on helping children understand their own experiences of bullying, reflect upon their own behaviour and learn how to improve it. The pupil-led anti-bullying approaches presented show you how you need to find out children's experiences of bullying first, and then consult with children and staff to develop, implement and evaluate an intervention. There is a wealth of knowledge from the children which can help you learn about their experiences of bullying and how to resolve it. Interestingly, all of the scenarios I have used to address bullying with children have derived entirely from children's own experiences.

Support for pupils to resolve bullying should focus on encouraging children to reflect on their reaction to bullying, consider a range of alternative responses and decide on which ones are likely to be the most effective and respectful. Children can respectfully challenge one another and decide on what would be the most effective response to bullying whilst working together in a group. Once you have supported pupils to enhance their understanding of bullying and developed effective strategies to resolve it, bring children who are in conflict with one another into discussions. Focus on understanding the underlying reasons behind the conflict. Use this knowledge to decide what the most effective approaches will be and ensure the children involved have input into deciding how their bullying will be dealt with.

All children are affected by bullying and ought to be directly involved in helping to resolve it, although they need support from adults to do so. Expecting children to simply intervene to stop bullying underestimates how affected by bullying they are and how vulnerable they can be to bullying if they intervene without having the skills, knowledge and support to resolve it effectively. Teach children how to internally and externally challenge their negative thoughts and feelings in response to their maltreatment. Once they have done this, support them to develop more effective ways of constructing and responding to their bullying so they can actively resist the power of individuals who are abusive towards them. The strategies in this book can be used to help equip children to develop their skills to successfully address bullying. Children who have been involved in pupil-led interventions have improved their understanding of themselves and others, developed skills in controlling their anger, have found positive outlets for their emotions, and have gained healthier relationships with staff and their peers. These interpersonal skills can help equip children to deal with bullying throughout their lifespan, for example, when they move from primary school to secondary school.

'Mentoring for "Bullies"'

Mentoring for children who persistently engage in bullying has been discussed to help children who engage in bullying refrain from doing so, and learn how to interact with their peers and teachers more respectfully. To provide mentoring, meet with mentees regularly; teach them how to behave more considerately; help enhance their perspective of other pupils and colleagues; and support them to make informed decisions about their behaviour. Unlike restorative approaches, mentoring specifically focuses on equipping children with the understanding and skills necessary to improve their behaviour and engage in self-development over a period of time rather than just trying to bring about peace between those who are in conflict with one another.

A 'system of dialogue' to improve unacceptable behaviour

Children who are being persistently punished are showing us that the disciplinary system schools usually use tends not to improve their behaviour. Is it surprising that forcing children to sit in isolation booths for several days or giving them frequent detentions rarely improves their behaviour or sense of morality? Instead it often makes children feel bored and angry: two of the main contributors to bullying. Encourage children to reflect on their behaviour and develop their morality to prevent the vicious cycle of abuse.

A 'system of dialogue' which draws upon the voice of pupils has been suggested as a more productive and effective means of improving children's behaviour. Such an approach involves meeting regularly with pupils who persistently misbehave to find out why they are misbehaving, and help them learn that their behaviour is unacceptable and develop more appropriate means of behaving and interacting with others. Teach children who misbehave how to behave more respectfully. Sometimes children may relapse into their usual behaviour but with encouragement and guidance they are more likely to improve. Consult with children to learn how systems which deal with unacceptable behaviour can be improved to instil a greater sense of justice and reduce children's feelings of victimization.

Combat bullying between pupils and staff

A holistic approach to bullying should not just focus on school practitioners as people who have a duty to stop bullying but also as individuals who can be bullied by pupils and colleagues, and as individuals who can engage in bullying pupils and colleagues. Reflect on how you speak with pupils and reprimand them. This book has argued that school staff need to provide a good example to pupils through how they behave and interact with them. Discuss with pupils and colleagues what children learn from staff about bullying based on their observations of how staff interact with pupils and colleagues. If children witness teachers humiliating and targeting children they may replicate this behaviour. In order to encourage children to refrain from bullying we need to ensure that they are not observing staff being bullied, or 'picking on' pupils.

Develop 'healthy relationships' in your schools between pupils, and pupils and staff. This means having more respectful interactions with one another rather than just refraining from bullying. You could have a 'healthy relationships' policy or incorporate this into your anti-bullying policy. A 'healthy relationships' policy would include guidance and examples of how pupils, and pupils and staff should interact respectfully and also outline what interactions are unacceptable. Staff also need to be supported to deal with bullying they may experience from pupils. Your school's anti-bullying policy should include information on what behaviours constitute the bullying of pupils by staff, and the bullying of staff by pupils. There should also be recommendations on how to deal with this. Collaborate with pupils and staff to develop this policy so the examples and recommendations are directly relevant to the specific issues you have in your school. It is important that school practitioners are not bullied by colleagues and managers so that they can effectively support pupils. Furthermore, it would be good practice to improve how teachers communicate with one another, and help them understand and combat bullying that can occur between staff. School managers should speak with colleagues to find out what support staff need to tackle bullying effectively which will help 'empower practitioners'.

'Empathetic understanding'

Pupils need to enhance their understanding of one another's perspectives by learning more about the viewpoints of others. Ask children why the person they are in conflict with is behaving in ways that cause them distress. Help them find out what is motivating them and what they are hoping to gain from bullying. From developing 'empathetic understanding' between pupils you can more effectively resolve the problems and develop healthier relationships. Support pupils and staff to understand the perspectives of other pupils and staff to whom they have caused distress and consider what they can do to help them. Encourage open dialogue amongst pupils and school practitioners about bullying.

An anti-bullying advisory group (ABAG) which involves both pupils and staff has been suggested as a way of developing a core team who work together to tackle bullying. This group will improve how you deal with bullying and your resources for tackling it. You can enhance the input of children by showing them what they can improve in school and how they can effectively articulate their voice. This approach can help children to 'take responsibility' for dealing with bullying in their school. It can also be used to improve the way your school understands and responds to bullying. Furthermore, it would be beneficial for schools to have a colleague or an external expert on bullying who focuses entirely on listening to, and tackling, children's experiences of bullying. The knowledge gained from working with children to resolve bullying can be used to improve how schools understand and deal with bullying. This would contribute to a proactive rather than reactive approach to addressing bullying and would ensure children's views are listened to.

Involving parents is likely to improve the effectiveness of your approach to tackling the multi-faceted nature of bullying. Furthermore, it can help you understand and address systemic bullying and the broader issues which contribute to bullying beyond the pupil and school practitioner level. It has been suggested how you can collaborate with a group of parents to enhance understanding of bullying between pupils, and pupils and teachers, and develop effective strategies to resolve these issues. If parents do not engage with this initiative then you could meet with parents individually to learn about how the school can work with them more effectively and what you can do to help them get more involved in combatting issues associated with bullying.

Continuous development

The new approaches to understand and tackle bullying based on empirical research in this book have demonstrated how you can develop evidence-based interventions in your school to deal with pupils' specific issues.

It has been outlined how teachers can continuously develop their knowledge about bullying and share this with colleagues. Strategies to embed teaching and learning for pupils about bullying into the curriculum have been outlined. As a school practitioner you have access to a wide range of knowledge and resources from the pupils and practitioners in your school, and this book has shown you how you to effectively access these to deal with the current issues your pupils have with bullying.

Directions for Future Development

Although *The Teacher's Guide to Resolving School Bullying* has researched systemic bullying, bullying between teachers and pupils, and disciplinary systems in school for dealing with unacceptable behaviour and bullying, there is still a scant amount of research in these areas. We need a better understanding of what to do to prevent 'vulnerable groups' being targeted, reduce bullying between pupils and teachers, and help them develop more respectful relationships. We also need to learn how to improve systems in school for dealing with unacceptable behaviour which enhance children's morality and that are more equitable than traditional means of punishment.

Further research is needed on the functions bullying serves and more effective strategies are needed to resolve this issue. Anti-bullying interventions should focus more on how to develop children's agency and their ability to make informed decisions, and for peers and staff to establish an organized network of support to combat bullying. There also needs to be additional research and more substantial strategies on how to encourage all members of the school community to work together to tackle bullying and improve the school system. Learning more about pupils' experiences of bullying, and collaborating with pupils and staff to combat it, is central to understanding the complexity of bullying and developing strategies to resolve it.

Policy implications

This book has demonstrated that policy makers need to improve their understanding of bullying rather than simply relying on the traditional approach, which has restricted our ability to understand bullying and address its complex nature. Policy makers need to improve their recommendations on how schools should respond to unacceptable behaviour. A 'system of dialogue' and 'Mentoring for "Bullies"' have been recommended to improve children's behaviour and sense of morality. Anti-bullying policy would benefit from improving understanding of bullying between pupils and teachers, and this should be included in recommendations of good practice for how to understand and deal with bullying. It would also be beneficial to consider how pupils, and pupils and staff, can interact more respectfully with one another, and develop 'healthier relationships' and 'empathetic understanding'. More research needs to be commissioned which pays substantial attention to children's experiences of bullying and consults with pupils and staff to effectively tackle it. If policy makers improve their understanding of the complexity of bullying and embrace the strategies in this book then the entire school culture would improve so children can thrive without the unnecessary harm that bullying causes.

Summary

The foundations of this book have been derived from children's views and experiences of the complexity of bullying to enhance your understanding and resources to tackle it effectively. This approach contrasts with the traditional approach which is over-reliant on statistics and does not thoroughly address the underlying issues of bullying. This book has presented a multi-faceted model of understanding and tackling bullying between pupils, bullying between pupils and teachers, and bullying at the systemic level. The key themes and strategies have been outlined. These have included: understanding bullying as a spectrum; understanding and addressing bullying which achieves peer approval; pupil-led anti-bullying interventions; 'Mentoring for "Bullies"' and how a 'system of dialogue' can improve children's behaviour. In addition, the following issues have been addressed: the importance of combating bullying between pupils and school staff; how you can develop 'empathetic understanding' between pupils, and pupils and staff; and advice on how you can continually develop your knowledge and strategies for tackling bullying. Finally, directions for future research and implications for policy have been outlined.

Appendix 1

Characteristics of School Bullying

The following aspects and characteristics of bullying involve different severities which range from mild to severe, and include 'grey' areas as well as those which are clearly bullying.

Feelings Associated with Bullying

Feelings occur as a consequence of a negative interaction/s with an individual/group. The following distressing feelings may persist after the maltreatment has occurred:

- Hurt.
- Frightened (for example, of violence).
- Humiliated.
- Anxious.
- Suicidal.
- Picked on/out.
- Inferior (not as good as others).

Clearly Bullying

Aggressive acts (physical or psychological) which are: repeated, intentional and involve a clear imbalance of power, whereby the victim has less power than the bully (Olweus 1993).

Forms of Bullying
Verbal

- Name-calling such as 'big ears' which upsets an individual is considered as bullying but individuals may conceal their distress.

- Being persistently called negative names such as 'fatty' which can be perpetrated by the same individuals or different people.

- Teasing someone in a negative way that ridicules them, for example, about their physical appearance, sexual orientation or ability. Teasing might be construed as amusing but can be associated with suicide.

Physical

- Pushing: Can be accidental or intentional.

- Kicking: A form of violence.

- Fighting/quarrelling: What experiences came before the conflict?

- Violence: Can have psychological side-effects. Does it cause fear?

- Hitting an individual: Why would someone hit someone else? Possibly for self-defence but they are still harming another individual.

- Beating an individual up.

Psychological

- Humiliation.

- Threats of physical violence.

- Ridicule.

Relational

- Being ostracized: Being left out, feeling alone, being pushed out of a group, having 'no one to play with', but what if an individual wants to be alone? It is necessary to look at the context and if the individual feels distressed as a consequence

- Preferences towards particular peer groups: To what extent is this normal/healthy and is a matter of who people choose to be friends with? When is it ostracism?

- Bullied by friends: Are they 'arguing' or bullying each other?

Teachers Bullying Pupils

- Being called 'stupid' in front of the class.

- Ridicule/Public ridicule: Consider the context and if the person felt ridiculed.

- Humiliation.

- A teacher perceived as abusing their power: Consider how this happens.

- Feeling 'picked on' for academic work: Is the teacher trying to encourage them, show them they could do better, or victimizing them? Explore the interaction.

- 'Unfair punishments': Do certain children feel unfairly targeted for punishments?

- Shouting at children: Explore what happened, what was said, who was it targeted at, an individual or group? Did children find it distressing?

Pupils Bullying Teachers

Many of the characteristics at the pupil–pupil level can also be experienced by teachers from pupils. Some specific behaviours pupils may engage in to bully their teachers include:

- Insults.

- Mockery.

- Pushing.

- Swearing.

Systemic (Institutional/Societal Factors)

- Oppression: Rejection of one's identity and sense of self, and suppression of one's 'voice'.

- Abuse: Bullying overlaps with abuse and is not neatly separate from it.

- Institutional factors. These can influence one's position in school, for example, streaming.

- Social class: Discriminated against for belonging to a certain social class.

- Gender: Treated unfavourably because of gender and/or sexual orientation, for example, marginalized for being LGBT.

- Intellectual ability: Discriminated against for having a learning difficulty or learning disabilities.

- Racism: Treated unfavourably because of ethnic origin.

Definition of School Bullying

Bullying involves maltreatment which ranges from mild to severe. The individual feels it is difficult to defend themselves, but there does not have to be a clearly defined power imbalance for bullying to occur. These negative experiences vary in severity; there are clear forms of bullying and 'grey' areas. Bullying includes forms that are verbal (for example, name-calling), psychological (for example, humiliation), physical (for example, being hit) and relational (for example, ostracism). Occasional name-calling or teasing that does not upset an individual is a 'grey' area which is not automatically considered as bullying, but it is not safe to assume that mild name-calling and teasing is not bullying. Teasing and name-calling which cause distress are considered to be on a spectrum of bullying. However, individuals may conceal their distress so further investigation is needed to find out if bullying is present. Individuals may intentionally or unconsciously engage in bullying.

Children's perceptions of what constitutes bullying vary, although there are some experiences that most would identify as bullying. When individuals are bullied their behaviour often becomes more closely observed, their differences are highlighted and they become increasingly pressured to conform. Consequently, once people are targeted, they can become susceptible to further bullying.

Most children do not report bullying because they are frightened that it will escalate; consequently they usually feel entrapped. Children who engage in bullying or who are victimized often do not label themselves as a 'bully' or 'victim' because they feel the way the terms are traditionally used stigmatize them and do not consider the complexities involved. It is therefore important to investigate beyond the 'bully' and 'victim' labels to consider the nuances and underlying issues which contribute to bullying. However, there are cases when children who persistently engage in bullying or are frequently victimized are likely to be labelled as 'bullies' or 'victims', for example, by pupils and teachers.

Furthermore, children do not tend to label themselves as 'bystanders' who simply observe the bullying process, and are more adversely affected by bullying, and involved in it, than most research typically considers.

Bullying can be persistent but does not have to be, particularly if it causes distress between individuals such as fear of repeated aggression. Bullying can happen in any relationship, for example, between friends. Systemic bullying is where certain children are distressed because they belong to a stigmatized group, for example, if children in the lowest stream are upset because they think they are perceived as 'thick'. Systemic bullying can underly bullying between pupils, and pupils and staff as individuals may reinforce institutional and societal inequalities by victimizing those positioned as 'vulnerable', for example victimizing children with learning difficulties.

Multi-Faceted Model of School Bullying

Figure 1 depicts the multi-faceted model of bullying which considers the messiness and nuances of bullying presented in this book.

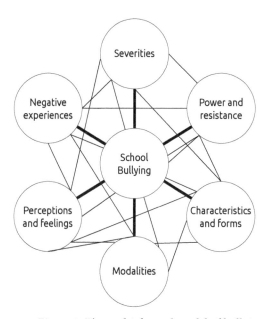

Figure 1: The multi-faceted model of bullying

This diagram takes into consideration the following factors: negative experiences; power and resistance; characteristics and forms; modalities (i.e. bullying involving pupils, pupils and staff, and at the systemic level); perceptions and feelings; and different severities. The bold lines link bullying with these factors. The lines which are not in bold show how the factors inter-link with each other.

Examples of How Themes Inter-Link

- *Severities*: There are different severities of negative experiences and modalities of bullying that children experience, which range from 'grey' to clearly bullying by pupils, by staff and at the systemic level.

- *Negative experiences*: Negative experiences, for example, vary depending on the modalities and forms of bullying.

- *Modalities*: The power which is exercised over individuals varies depending on the modalities of bullying which can be bullying by pupils, by teachers or at the systemic level.

- *Characteristics and forms*: Different forms of bullying, for example, name-calling, vary depending on severity.

- *Perceptions and feelings*: How individuals feel and perceive bullying is influenced by how much power operates over them and how much resistance they can exercise.

- *Power and resistance*: The extent to which people feel power is abused over them varies according to the severity of bullying. The more power is exercised over individuals, the more closely they are scrutinized and targeted, which increasingly restricts their opportunities to resist being victimized.

Staff Training

The Complexity of School Bullying and What to Do about It

These are the PowerPoint notes I have used to train school practitioners about bullying. The information in Chapter 5 will help you expand on these notes which you can use to provide training to colleagues.

Aim and Objectives

Aim

To enhance understanding of the complexity of bullying and develop effective strategies to reduce it.

Objectives

- Recognize what constitutes bullying.

- Understand why children engage in bullying.

- Learn about evidence-based approaches to tackle bullying.

- Consider what anti-bullying approaches you can apply and develop in your role.

What is Bullying?

- Aggression: Repeated, intentional and a clear power imbalance (Olweus 1993).

- No universally agreed definition (Chan 2009).

- 'I didn't mean it'; 'only joking'.
- One act: Fear and distress afterwards.
- Friends: Where is the power imbalance?
- Characteristics of bullying, for example teasing.
- Feelings and perceptions – 'grey' areas.
- Is teasing bullying?

Is Teasing Bullying?

- Traditional definition.
- Teasing in a 'grey' zone – lightens mood but can be distressing and even lead to suicide (Morita 1996).
- Bullying as a spectrum from mild to severe.
- Feelings are important.
- 'Grey' areas: Banter, name-calling.
- Certainty?
- Complexity: Laughing, saying it's not bullying?
- Why do children bully?

Why do Children Bully?

- Popularity – social power but unstable.
- Boredom – lack of control, bullying provides entertainment.
- Because they are bullied.
- Jealousy – want what someone else has got.
- Overtly aggressive males: 'bullies'.
- Reinforce group norms: functional.
- Although individuals might learn to bully through noticing that children can gain social approval for bullying, individuals can exercise agency and decide to interact with their peers more respectfully.

The 'Bullying' Label

- 'Grey' areas: Banter, friends?
- Cyber-bullying – anonymity? Widespread.
- Homophobia: Vulnerability, law.
- Sexualized bullying.
- Racism: For example, Islamophobia.
- Workplace bullying.
- Research findings from Nassem (2017)
  - Individuals who have learning difficulties and/or who are identified by their peers as 'different' are more susceptible to being bullied.
  - Children experience systemic bullying because of the societal and institutional inequalities in school which school practitioners and pupils can reinforce.
  - There can be power struggles and bullying between pupils and teachers which need to be addressed.
  - Children from particularly economically deprived working-class backgrounds who valued approval from their peers above their teachers were often bullied by their peers and teachers and experienced systemic bullying. This was particularly found in males but was also experienced by some females from this group.
- Student–teacher bullying.
- Gender and social class.

Teachers' Role

- Teachers are social engineers of change in the classroom (Chan 2009).
- Complex positioning of school staff.
- Teachers should feel confident and equipped to deal with bullying (Ofsted 2012).

- Do you feel confident and equipped to handle bullying?

Consider...

- Pupils may not report being bullied.
- Why might a bullied child not report it?
- How can you help a child if they don't report bullying?
- What if you think someone is being bullied but they don't?
- Pupils may lose social power if they stop bullying; what can we replace this with?

Signs of Bullying

- Behavioural: For example not eating, school absence, signs of anxiety, developing a stammer.
- Social: Ostracized – Socially withdraw.
- Under-performance with work.
- Being teased and tormented.
- Being blamed for incidents.
- 'No one likes you'.

Department for Education (2017)

- Schools – measures to prevent bullying: Legal duty.
- Not marked down for having bullying: Resolution.
- Make it easy for pupils to report bullying.
- Pupils aware of how they can prevent bullying.
- Parents: Procedural awareness and confident to report.
- Evaluate and update your approach to new technology.
- Discuss difference: Prejudiced language is unacceptable.
- Work with the wider community such as police.

- Disciplinary cases – fair and consistent.

How Schools Usually Deal with Bullying

- Anti-bullying policy.
- Refer to definition.
- Overt punishment.
- Contact with parents.
- Mediation.
- External expert.

Outline of a School Anti-Bullying Policy

- Definition, forms and symptoms of bullying.
- All staff to be alert to signs of bullying and act against it.
- Reported to principal; class teacher and parents informed.
- Victimized: Reassurance, support, build self-esteem.
- 'Bullies': Sanctions and inform parents/guardians.
- Warnings, stop playtimes, fixed and permanent exclusion.
- Focus on bullying in autumn, whole-school approach.

What Could Help School Practitioners?

- Training.
- Support: Colleagues and management.
- Trade unions.
- Reading and applying policies.
- Mentoring.
- Speak to pupils about bullying.
- Refer to anti-bullying policy.

Established Strategies
Staff-focused

- Extending control: Where bullying is likely.

- Stimulating environment: Beat boredom.

- Circle time and assemblies.

- KiVa (Hutchings and Clarkson 2017).

Pupil-focused

- Shared concern (Pikas 1989): Work with the peer group to find solutions.

- Anti-bullying ambassadors.

- Restorative justice.

- Assertiveness training for victims.

- Peer support: Befriending, mentoring, counselling.

- Mediation: Work with all parties to find solutions.

Recommendations

- Speak to the individual/s who are involved and listen.

- Holistic approach.

- Ask the victimized child: What do you want me to do? What do you want to happen? Clarify how you will move forwards.

- Discuss issues of bullying in class – influences everyone.

- Agree ground rules of how to be respectful with one another.

- 'Empathetic understanding': Between pupils, and between pupils and teachers.

- Deal with conflict when it occurs.

- Discuss how to develop 'healthy relationships': Between pupils, and between pupils and staff.

- Check bullying has not recurred, for example through regular meetings.

- Establish a pupil and staff ABAG.

- A 'system of dialogue' to deal with unacceptable behaviour.

'Mentoring for "Bullies"'

- No 'bullies' (Nassem 2012, 2017).

- Males, physically aggressive, learning difficulties.

- Do they want to change? Start from behaviour.

- Support to reflect and behave more respectfully: Agency.

- Aim to understand underlying reasons children bully.

- Weekly meetings, for example over two months with staff.

- Why did you behave the way you did? How did it make people feel and how can you behave more respectfully?

- Experiment: Different behaviours and outcomes; Role-play.

- Significant reductions in bullying and improved peer relations.

Working with Children to Resolve Bullying

- Child's voice central to understanding their experiences and effective interventions (Nassem 2017).

- Pupil-led anti-bullying assemblies.

- Strategies tailored to specific issues of pupils.

- Individual interviews with each child: Experiences.

- Focus groups with children about interventions.

- Focus groups with staff: Children's experiences and intervention.

- Observations, for example playground and classroom.

- Evaluation: Focus groups (staff and pupils).

Project Implementation

- Diaries: Emotional outlet.

- Understanding the perspectives of others.

- Understanding and dealing with our feelings, for example releasing anger.

- Considering alternative behaviours.

- Reflecting on own behaviours and how to behave more respectfully.

- Informed decisions and considering consequences.

- Group work to build self-esteem.

- Activities include: Role-play, discussions, reflection and diaries.

- Meeting together with children who are in conflict.

- Output of work, for example staff–pupil meetings, pupil-led anti-bullying assemblies.

Evaluation

- Significant reductions in bullying.

- Helping victimized children.

- Improved relations with peers.

- Responding respectfully to other pupils.

- Understanding and reflecting.

- Change is difficult.

Helpful Strategies

- Pupil-led approaches: Voice.

- 'Take responsibility': Institutional and individual.

- Support for children to change/improve.

- What support do colleagues need to tackle bullying?

- Draw upon different strategies for a tailored approach.

'Mentoring for "Bullies"'

Individualized Support

Each session of mentoring usually lasts about an hour but can be between 45 minutes and two hours depending on the child's engagement and the issues which are discussed. The details below aim to guide you to develop a mentoring programme tailored to the individual pupils you work with and adjusted to suit their needs.

Session 1: Introduction

Introduce yourself and the programme to the mentee. Ask them if they would like to have the mentoring, what they would like support with and how they would like you to help them. The support required will probably consist of improving how they are getting along with some of their peers and staff, and help to stop them getting into trouble by behaving more respectfully.

Reflect with the child on how their week has been, and how they have been getting along with pupils and staff. Find out from them the last time they had conflict with other pupils and/or staff in school, what happened and how they responded. Consider with them alternative ways of responding. Ask the child if it would be helpful for you to give them a diary so they can record events and use this as a tool to reflect on their thoughts and feelings with you. Discuss and agree what areas you will focus on in the following session when you will next meet.

Session 2: Strategies to Resolve Conflict

In this session recap with the mentee what has happened over the week since you last saw them and when they have been in conflict/ involved in bullying with other pupils and/or staff. Role-play with the mentee what happened. Alternate the roles you play so they can play themselves in one scenario and the person they are in conflict with in another scenario. Discuss how others responded to them and why they responded the way they did. Consider alternative and more respectful ways of responding and role-play these responses. This can help the child prepare to have more respectful conversations with pupils and/or staff, and you can suggest some ways they can respond more effectively. This approach is termed 'conflict resolution role-play' and can be used throughout the mentoring programme. You can also talk about what they would like to say to the people who bully them and how they feel about being bullied. Mini whiteboards or notecards can be used as resources for children to write their responses. If they don't want to write long sentences then just encourage them to write down key words to express themselves.

Session 3: Responding to Bullying

Discuss in more depth some of the salient issues you have talked about in the last session such as what the child would like to say to the people who bully them and what they would like help with. Continue to help prepare them to have productive conversations with pupils and staff who they are in conflict with and respectfully articulate their thoughts and feelings. Use the 'conflict resolution role-play' for children to reflect on how they can respond to disagreements more respectfully. Freeze-frame can also be used in the role-play where individuals stop at a certain part in their role-play to pause. After you have used freeze-frame reflect with the child on how they are responding and then role-play alternative ways they can behave.

Throughout this activity you can analyze the different ways they can respond to bullying. Discuss how they can interpret the behaviours of others differently, for example, what they can do instead of being extremely angry when someone insults them. You might want to ask them to pretend to be someone who they admire such as a famous footballer, and speak and act as if they are them in the session. When children pretend to be individuals who they admire they often become enthusiastic, confident and improve how they communicate. You can then remind them to channel their confidence and improved communication into their interactions with you throughout the mentoring sessions.

Session 4: Making Improvements

Review with the mentee what specifically they would like to have support with. Discuss with them why they behave the way they do and what they think they may be gaining and losing out on because of their behaviour. Ask them how they can achieve respect from their peers through more respectful behaviours. Support the mentee to further practice having effective and respectful conversations with staff and/or pupils with whom they are in conflict to discuss their disagreements and decide how to move forward. Use the 'conflict resolution role-play' so children can act out, and learn about, different perspectives. Discuss in more depth what they would like to say to the people who are bullying them and help them consider effective ways of thinking and responding to others when they feel upset or angry with them. Talk about, and agree on, what behaviour the mentee is going to try to improve next week such as speaking calmly to those who upset them rather than shouting.

Session 5: Consequences of Behaviour

Reflect on the progress that has been made so far and review behavioural targets agreed from the last session. Consider where there have been improvements and where more improvements can be made. Discuss in more depth how they can manage their anger and respond to conflict more peacefully. Support the child to consider making friends with other children outside of their immediate friendship circle. Talk about other pupils who have been aggressive at school and what has happened to them. Discuss likely consequences of their aggressive behaviour such as being excluded from school. Read the school's anti-bullying policy with the mentee. Ask them if they are experiencing any of these behaviours and what behaviours they are engaging in which might constitute bullying. Show them how they can effectively report and respond to bullying. Agree targets for how they can improve their behaviour which will be reviewed in the next session.

Session 6: Moving On

Discuss behavioural targets set last week and consider the extent to which they were achieved. Consider what has helped and hindered the achievements of their behavioural targets. Reflect on how to overcome obstacles in achieving their behavioural targets. Ask how the mentoring programme is progressing and help prepare the child for the mentoring coming to an end by discussing what other forms of support they can have in school. Expand the discussion on how to make friends with children outside of their friendship group. Find out if they have attempted to do this and how it is going. Review the child's behavioural targets for next week. Help prepare the child for having a joint meeting with another child who they are in conflict with. Before this session discuss with these children how they can respectfully express their thoughts and feelings about the problem, and respond respectfully if they feel upset and/or angry.

Session 7: Meeting with Pupils Who Are in Conflict with One Another

Inform the two children who are in conflict with one another that they are meeting to talk about how they are getting along and how they can get on better. If you have not met with the child you are bringing into the meeting before, then ensure you meet with them to help prepare them for the joint meeting. Ensure that children feel comfortable about attending this meeting. Encourage children to respectfully talk about why they are having disagreements and what the underlying issues are. Ask them how they are feeling about the conflict they are having. Deliberate and agree with children how they will interact with each other in future and what they will do differently as a result of their meeting. Consider if any future meetings with these children, or other pupils involved, need to be held to reduce any further tensions and conflict which may arise. These meetings are likely to be less confrontational if they are just held with two children who are in conflict with one another in each meeting, as well as the mediator.

Session 8: Endings

Review the child's experience of the mentoring, what went well, what did not go as well and how the sessions can be developed. Ask the mentee how they are and how they are getting along with other children. Discuss how they felt about the meeting with the child they were in conflict with and how they have been getting along with each other over the week. Reflect with them on how they are going to get along with other pupils and staff, how they are changing their behaviour and what aspects of trying to improve their behaviour they are finding difficult. Discuss endings and new beginnings and sources of support to help the child now the mentoring has finished. Summarize the main techniques the child can use to resolve conflict and practise these together.

Examples of Group Mentoring

Provide group mentoring sessions for about three to six pupils. You might want to facilitate group mentoring for mentees who are in the same friendship group to help you learn about and challenge norms within their peer group.

Session 1: Consequences of Aggressive Behaviour

Discuss why children may behave in unpleasant ways towards others and what they think they may gain from their behaviour. Ask the children to consider what the side-effects might be as a consequence of their behaviour for themselves or others. Talk about peer pressure and the positive and negative consequences of conforming to it or resisting it. Ask them if there is another child who is older than them who has behaved like them previously and what happened to them when they finished attending school. Reflect on what may happen to children who are excluded from school because of their aggressive behaviour and leave without any qualifications. Consider with pupils the consequences of their behaviour such as how it makes their target feel, how it impacts others in their class and what happens to the aggressor as a result of their behaviour. Set behavioural targets for next week.

Session 2: Responding to Conflict

Review the behavioural targets from last week, and to what extent they were achieved. Discuss with pupils how their week has been and if they have encountered any problems with other pupils and/or staff. Use the 'conflict resolution role-play' to help them learn how to respond more respectfully in future. Support pupils to enhance their communication skills, for example, by providing more eye contact and speaking more clearly.

Talk with children about why there is bullying. Most children will say that children bully to be popular and because they are bored. Help children consider these motivations and the positive and negative side-effects this behaviour has on other pupils. Analyze in more depth how children can achieve power in more positive ways than bullying. Develop individualized and group plans of how mentees can improve their behaviour and achieve peer approval through more positive means instead of bullying. Support children to set individual targets which will be reviewed in the following week to focus on how they will reduce their aggression and interact with their peers more respectfully.

Interview Questions for Children about Their Experiences of Bullying

Outline

- Welcome children and introduce yourself.

- No right or wrong answer: 'I want to know what you think.'

- Interview children individually or in a focus group.

- Explain the ethical matters which may arise from the research.

- If you are interviewing children in focus groups tell them that they should not discuss the personal information shared by others outside of the interview.

- Explain it is important that only one person speaks at a time.

- 'I want to ask you about bullying and how people get along with each other in school.'

- Note: Focus on covering the main themes in the interview schedule rather than ensuring that each question is asked in all of the interviews.

INTERVIEW QUESTIONS	FOLLOW-UP AND NOTES
Introduction	
What do you think of school?	Do you like/enjoy school? Why?
What do you think relationships are like in school?	Amongst pupils? Between pupils and teachers?
How do you feel you get along with other pupils? Teachers?	
Do you feel your views are listened to in school?	Can you express your feelings?
Experiences of Offline Bullying	
What kinds of bullying do children experience in school?	What do people say and/or do when they bully someone? For example, what name-calling have you heard in school?
How do people feel when they are bullied?	
Why do you think people bully others?	What might they get out of it?
Where does most bullying happen?	
Experiences of Cyberbullying	
What kinds of cyberbullying do children experience?	For example, having upsetting things said about them online, by phone or by text.
How do people feel when they experience cyberbullying?	
Why do you think people bully others through cyberbullying, for example on the internet or on mobile phones?	What might they get out of it?
Where does most cyberbullying happen?	For example, which websites, or by mobile phone?
What People Do about Bullying: Online and Offline	
What do people do when they are bullied?	For example, miss school, hit back. Does this help?
What do other pupils do when there is bullying?	
What do teachers do when there is bullying?	Playground supervisors, learning mentors, other school staff?
What do parents do when there is bullying?	What can they do?

Do people listen to those who report bullying?	Is bullying taken seriously?
Do you know if your school has an anti-bullying policy?	Where is it? Have you read it? Is it useful?

What People Can/Should Do about Bullying: Online and Offline

What can people who are being bullied do to stop it?	
What should people do when they are bullied?	Is this likely to be helpful?
Can people stop themselves from being bullied in school?	How? What can they do?
Is there anything you can do to stop bullying?	Others being bullied? You being bullied? What?
What can school staff, for example teachers or playground supervisors, do about bullying?	
What should be done about bullying in school?	Should more be done about bullying? What?
How should bullying be dealt with in school?	For example, punishment, restorative justice, empathy building.

Appendix 8

Interview Schedule with Staff about Children's Experiences of Bullying

Outline

- Welcome participants and introduce yourself.

- Explain ethical aspects of the research, for example, confidentiality (for staff being interviewed not to discuss the personal information shared outside the interview).

- No right or wrong answer: 'I want to know what you think.'

- 'I want to ask you about bullying and how people get along with each other in school.'

INTERVIEW QUESTIONS	FOLLOW-UP AND NOTES
Introduction	
How do pupils and school staff get along with each other?	Relationships between pupils and between pupils and teachers.
How are children's views listened to in school?	
Experiences of Offline Bullying	
What kinds of bullying do children experience in school?	What do people say and/or do when they bully someone? For example, what name-calling have you heard in school?
How do people feel when they are bullied?	
Why do you think people bully others?	What might they get out of it?
Where does most bullying happen?	

Experiences of Cyberbullying

What kinds of cyberbullying do children experience?

Having upsetting things said about them online, phone, text…

How do children feel when they experience cyberbullying?

Why do you think children bully others through cyberbullying, for example on the internet or mobile phones?

What might they get out of it?

Where does most cyberbullying happen?

For example, which websites, or by mobile phone?

What People Do about Bullying: Online and Offline

What do people do when they are bullied?

For example, miss school, hit back. Does this help?

What do other pupils do when there is bullying?

What do teachers do when there is bullying?

Playground supervisors, learning mentors, other school staff?

What helps school staff deal with bullying?

What makes it difficult?

What do parents do when there is bullying?

What can they do?

How seriously is bullying taken in school?

Does the school anti-bullying policy help deal with bullying?

How?

What People Can/Should Do about Bullying: Online and Offline

What can children who are being bullied do to stop it?

What should children do when they are bullied?

Is this likely to be helpful?

Can children stop themselves from being bullied in school?

How? What can they do?

Is there anything more you can do personally to stop bullying?

Position of school staff in school.

What can other school staff, for example teachers or playground supervisors, do about bullying?

How should bullying be dealt with in school?

Should more be done about bullying? What? For example, punishment, empathy building, mentoring.

Appendix 9

Intervention Questions for Children: Phase 1

QUESTIONS	FOLLOW-UP AND NOTES
Consequences of Strategies	
What strategies might not be helpful to those who are victimized?	
Are there any ways that bullying is dealt with in school which might make it worse?	What are these? Why?
If we punish 'bullies' how do we do this, what is likely to happen?	Could refer to anti-bullying policy.
What Would Help Stop Bullying?	
What would help stop bullying in school?	
What ideas have we got to help staff stop bullying?	Would they help stop bullying? What issues might arise from these?
What Work Can We Do to Help?	
How can we help stop people bullying others?	
What work can we do in this project to help stop bullying?	
What can we do to support those who are victimized?	
How do we encourage those who observe bullying do something to help?	What work can we do in this project to help them do more?

How can we help 'bullies' understand how they are making other people feel?

Would this help them stop? Why?

How can we help children who are upset about bullying feel better?

How can we encourage those who are bullied to help stop the bullying?

If we improved the way people, for example 'bullies' and 'victims', communicate, would this help?

How can we help children feel it's OK to be different?

Reflection on Implementation of Ideas

If we implement your ideas, what do you think would happen?

What is good about this idea, what might the problems be with this?

What about your anti-bullying procedures?

[Read out loud selected parts of the school's anti-bullying policy.] Would this help stop the bullying? Would those who are victimized perceive this as helpful? Is it likely to encourage other people to help? Is there anything we can add here to improve how bullying is dealt with?

What do you think we can work on together to help?

↓ Appendix 10

Intervention Questions for Children: Phase 2

INTERVIEW QUESTIONS	FOLLOW-UP AND NOTES
Consequences/Responsibility	
What can we do to help those who bully others realize the impact of their behaviour on others?	Consequences?
What can be done for children to realize the difference between joking and bullying?	
How can we help pupils understand the perspective of others more?	Share feelings?
How can we help stop people retaliating when they are being bullied?	
Taking Bullying Seriously	
How can we encourage staff to take bullying more seriously?	A priority?
What can we do to support school staff and pupils to be more alert to bullying?	Deal with bullying before it goes too far?
How can we ensure pupils don't get in trouble for reporting bullying?	Embarrassed? Victimized more?
Support to Deal with Bullying	
Would additional support to deal with bullying in school help and what could this be?	For example, someone to deal specifically with bullying? Support for you individually/in groups?

Would it help if you made posters about bullying and what to do about it?

Would it be beneficial for school staff and pupils to meet together to talk about bullying in small groups?

How could we do this? Which school staff should it involve?

Would encouraging 'bullies' and 'victims' to talk to each other about the bullying help?

How can this be done in a supportive way?

Would an assembly led by pupils about the seriousness of bullying and what to do about bullying be useful?

How can we go about this?

Would writing stories about your experiences of bullying and sharing it with others help?

How?

Would a diary where you regularly record what has happened to you and how you feel help?

Share with researcher? Staff? Anyone else?

Managing Our Feelings

How can we make it so bullying doesn't upset us so much?

How can we make 'bullies' feel better so they don't bully others?

For example, less angry?

What can we help people do instead of bullying others?

How can we let go of bad feelings we might have when we are bullied?

How can we help children realize when they are being bullied?

Relationships

Would you like to be separated from those who bully you?

Why? If the answer is 'yes', then how?

How can we help pupils who are bullied feel more included?

How can we help those who are bullied not withdraw from social activities?

How can we teach people to help others who are bullied?

How can we help children have more healthy friendships?

Improved interactions, more respect?

How can we support children to accept those who are different from them more?

Online Bullying

How can we help children not bully others online?

How can we help children deal with bullying online?

Appendix 11

Intervention Questions for Staff

QUESTIONS	FOLLOW-UP AND NOTES
What Would Help Stop Bullying?	
What would help stop school bullying?	
What would help support staff to stop bullying?	What issues might arise from these suggestions?
Consequences of Strategies	
What strategies might not be helpful to those who are victimized?	
If we punish 'bullies' how do we do this? What is likely to happen as a consequence?	Could refer to anti-bullying policy.
What Work Can We Do to Help?	
What work can we do in this project to help stop bullying?	
What can we do in this project to help those who are victimized?	
How do we encourage those who observe bullying do something to help?	What can we do to support them to do more?
How can we help 'bullies' realize how they are making other people feel?	Would this encourage them to stop? Why?
How can we support children who are upset about bullying to feel better?	

How can we encourage children to stop bullying others?

If we improved the way people, for example 'bullies' and 'victims', communicate, would this help?

How can we help people feel it's OK to be different?

Reflection on Implementation of Ideas

If we implement your ideas, what do you think would happen?

What is good about this idea, what might the problems be with this?

What about your anti-bullying procedures?

[Refer to parts of anti-bullying policy and read them out loud.] Would this help stop the bully? Would those who are victimized perceive this as useful? Is this likely to encourage other people to help? Is there anything we can add here to improve how bullying is dealt with?

What do you think we can work on together in this project?

↓

Anti-Bullying Group Sessions

Prior to delivering these sessions, speak to children and staff about children's experiences of bullying and about how to design an intervention to help them tackle bullying. This information can be formally accessed through facilitating focus groups with children and staff. You can also provide individual interviews with children about their experiences of bullying if you want to investigate the issue in more depth. Once you have data from children and staff about bullying you can use a thematic analysis to investigate what the main areas are which have arisen. From analyzing the main themes of the issues which have arisen you can start to develop ideas of how you can implement an intervention tailored to children's specific problems with bullying.

Although working with staff will enhance the impact of the work, the following details of the sessions will help you even if you do not have adequate support from your colleagues. The information below aims to provide for you a format which you can adjust according to the specific issues your pupils have.

Session 1: Introduction

Meet with children to define the scope of how the project will proceed. Discuss with children what you have broadly found from speaking to them, and your ideas for implementing the intervention, and agree what you will be working on. Sit with children in a circle to remove the sense of hierarchy and help them effectively communicate with one another. Give children a diary and ask them to write in their diary at home regularly about how they are getting along with pupils and staff in school, what has happened and how they feel about it. Talk about confidentiality and state that children should not share with others what is discussed in the session. Ask children how they respond to conflict and how they feel when they are bullied. Talk about why they respond the way they do, the consequences of their response and what the most effective way to respond would be. Agree what you will work on next week, how long the project will last and how you will evaluate the project, for example, by interviewing pupils and staff. Talk about what output children would like to produce at the end of the project. Suggest examples such as pupils designing and delivering an assembly, children writing about their experiences of bullying to be shared with the school community, meeting with staff to feed back what they have learnt, and/or advice and guidance to resolve bullying. Meet with staff after the session to keep them informed about the project and ask for any support if required.

Session 2: What Can You Do about Bullying?

Discuss with children in more depth their recent experiences of bullying and how they responded. Reflect on how they might have hurt others by their behaviour and consider how they can behave more respectfully and empathically. Use 'conflict resolution role-play' for children to demonstrate their experiences of bullying, how they felt and how they responded. This also involves children acting out alternative ways they can feel and respond to the bullying. Consider with children the most effective ways they can respond to the bullying they have role-played and discussed. Ask children to reflect on what they are hoping to achieve from these sessions and agree what you will work on next week.

Session 3: Responding to Bullying

Discuss recent problems children have had with their peers over the past week and how they have responded to them. Consider how children can interpret and respond to their bullying effectively. Ask how children are getting along with their diaries.

Role-play with children how they can talk respectfully to those who bully them, explain how they feel, what they might do about the problem if it continues, and that they want the maltreatment to stop. Bring in the school's anti-bullying policy, and read and review this with children. Ask children what they think about their school's anti-bullying policy, how it might help and how it can be improved. Find out how children report bullying to staff and discuss with them how to report bullying effectively. Role-play how bullying can be reported effectively to staff. Talk to children about how they feel about themselves when they are bullied and how they can maintain their self-esteem and feel better about themselves when they are being bullied. Raise the question: why do children bully? Start to consider how to include children who might be difficult to get along with. Decide what output you will use to showcase what children have learnt to others in school and outline how you will do this.

Session 4: Including Others

Talk about how children have been getting along with others over the past week, if there has been any conflict and how they have responded. Ask if they have tried to include other pupils who are left out, what happened, what was difficult and what went well. Consider with the group how they can include others more and how children who are left out might feel. Notecards can be useful for children to write down or draw how ostracized children might feel. Talk about, and agree, what each child will do to include others who are ostracized. Reflect with children on what they are learning and what they would like to develop further. Discuss in more detail what the output will be of the anti-bullying work and what you need to do to prepare for the output.

Session 5: Releasing Bad Feelings

Review children's recent experiences of bullying, how they reacted and how to respond respectfully in future. Address in more depth with children how to let go of bad feelings from bullying and feel better. Consider with children what improvements they have made, if there have been any changes to their behaviour and, if so, what has changed. Ask children what areas they are finding difficult to work on and where they would like more support. Address in more detail what children can say and do to help those who are bullied. Start to design the output of the anti-bullying work. Establish which staff and/or students will participate in the project output, for example, pupils might want to feed back what they have done to their school council. Help children set targets to improve how they respond to bullying and help others who are victimized, to be addressed in the following session.

Session 6: Preparing Output of Anti-Bullying Work

Review children's behavioural targets and to what extent they were achieved. Review experiences of conflict children have had since the

last session, how they have responded and can effectively respond. Expand
your discussion on how children can help others who are bullied. Set
behavioural targets for the following week and remind children to bring
their diaries for you to read next week. Consider how children can
show what they have learnt and use this to help others, for example,
through an assembly. Work on the anti-bullying output and what will
be presented. Reflect with children on what they have learnt and what
they are doing differently to address bullying.

Session 7: Pupil-Led Anti-Bullying Output

Collect children's diaries and help them prepare to present their output
to staff and/or students. Use this to showcase the following: what
children have done; what they have learnt; what they would like to say
about bullying; what they would like staff and pupils to do more/less of
with bullying; how they want to help others; and how they would like
their work to be developed. Evaluate the intervention with children and
staff and use this knowledge to improve how pupils and staff perceive
and respond to bullying.

Appendix 13

Evaluation Questions for Children

- What did you think about the work we have done?
- What went well?
- What didn't go so well?
- What did you find useful?
- What have you learned?
- Has it had an impact on your behaviour?
- Has it had an impact on the other children involved in the project? Has it had an impact on other children not involved in the project?
- Would you do this again?
- Do you think it has had an impact on staff? How?
- What would you like to see more of?
- How do you think the work could be developed/improved?
- Would you have liked more staff involved?
- What would you like to happen next?
- Do you feel you can handle bullying better now? How would you handle bullying differently now?

Appendix 14

Evaluation Questions for Staff

- What do you think about the work we have done?
- What impact do you think it has had on the children involved?
- How have you found it?
- Do you think it has had an impact on staff?
- How could this be improved?
- Would you do a project like this again?

References

Bandura, A., Ross, D. and Ross, S.A. (1961) 'Transmission of aggression through imitation of aggressive models.' *Journal of Abnormal and Social Psychology 63,* 575–582.

Bansel, P.B., Davies, B., Laws, C. and Linnell, S. (2009) 'Bullies, bullying and power in the context of schooling.' *British Journal of Sociology of Education 30,* 1, 59–69.

BBC News (2017) 'Childhood bullying anxiety declines over time study says.' 4 October. Accessed on 20/08/2018 at www.bbc.co.uk/news/health-41503014.

Boulton, M.J. (1994) 'Understanding and Preventing Bullying in the Junior Playground.' In P.K. Smith and S. Sharp (eds) *School Bullying: Insights and Perspectives.* London: Routledge.

Bourdieu, P. (1990) *The Logic of Practice.* Cambridge: Polity.

Caravita, S.C.S., Di Blasio, P. and Salmivalli, C. (2009) 'Unique and interactive effects of empathy and social status on involvement in bullying.' *Social Development 18,* 1, 140–63.

Chan, J.H. (2009) 'Where is the imbalance?' *Journal of School Violence 8,* 2, 177–190.

Cullingford, C. and Brown, G. (1995) 'Children's perceptions of victims and bullies.' *Education 3-13, 23,* 2, 11–17.

Department for Education (2017) *Preventing and Tackling Bullying: Advice for Headteachers, Staff and Governing Bodies.* London: DfE.

Department for Education (2018) *Keeping Children Safe in Education: Statutory guidance for schools and colleges.* London: DfE.

De Pear, S. and Garner, P. (1996) 'Tales from the Exclusion Zone: The Views of Teachers and Pupils' Exclusion from School'. In E. Blyth and J. Milner (eds) *Exclusion from School: Inter-professional Issues for Policy and Practice.* London: Routledge.

Duncan, N. (1999) *Sexual Bullying.* London: Routledge.

Epp, P.J. and Watkinson, A.M. (1997) 'Preface.' In R.J. Epp and A.M. Watkinson (eds) *How Schools Hurt Children.* London: Falmer Press.

Equality and Human Rights Commission (2018) *Protected Characteristics.* Manchester: Equality and Human Rights Commission. Accessed on 21/08/18 at www.equalityhumanrights.com/en/equality-act/protected-characteristics.

Foucault, M. (1979) *Discipline and Punish: The Birth of the Prison.* London: Penguin.

Foucault, M. (1980) *Michel Foucault: Power/Knowledge: Selected Interviews and other Writings.* Brighton: Harvester.

French, A., Lowe, R., and Nassem, E. (2018) 'Pupil-led research in primary schools.' *Education 3-13, 47, 2,* 148–161.

Frey, K.S. (2005) 'Gathering and communicating information about school bullying: Overcoming secrets and lies.' *Health Education 105,* 6, 409–413.

Gumpel, T., Zioni-Koren, V. and Bekerman, Z. (2014), 'An ethnographic study of participant roles in school bullying.' *Aggressive Behaviour 40,* 3, 214–228.

Hepburn, A. (1997) 'Teachers and secondary school bullying: A postmodern discourse analysis.' *Discourse and Society 9,* 1, 639–665.

Hodkinson, P. and Bloomer, M. (2001) 'Dropping out of further education: Complex causes and simplistic policy assumptions.' *Research Papers in Education 16,* 2, 117–140.

Hutchings, J. and Clarkson, S. (2017) *KiVa Antibullying Program.* Bangor: Centre for Evidence Based Early Intervention.

Impett, A.E., Sorsoli, L., Schooler, D., Henson, J.M. and Tolman, D.L. (2008) 'Girls' relationship authenticity and self-esteem across adolescence.' *Developmental Psychology 44,* 3, 722–733.

Jacobson, R.B. (2010) 'Narrating characteristics: The making of a school bully.' *Interchange 41,* 1, 255–283.

Kemmis, S. and Wilkinson, M. (1998) 'Participatory Action Research and the Study of Practice.' In B. Atwech, S. Kemmis and P. Weeks (eds) *Action Research in Practice: Partnerships for Social Justice in Education.* London: Routledge.

Kousholt, K. and Fisker, T.B. (2015) 'Approaches to reduce bullying in schools – a critical analysis from the viewpoint of first- and second-order perspectives on bullying.' *Children & Society 29,* 6, 593–603.

Kyriacou, C., and Zuin, A. (2015) 'Cyberbullying of teachers by students on YouTube: Challenging the image of teacher authority in the digital age.' *Research Papers in Education 31,* 255–273.

Leat, D., Reid A. and Lofthouse, R. (2015) 'Teachers' experiences of engagement with and in educational research: What can be learned from teachers' views.' *Oxford Review of Education 41,* 2, 270–286.

Lee, C. (2006) 'Exploring teachers' definitions of bullying.' *Educational and Behavioural Difficulties 11,* 1, 61–75.

Littlechild, B. (2003) *An Evaluation of the Implementation of a Restorative Justice Approach in a Residential Unit for Young People in Hertfordshire.* Hatfield: University of Hertfordshire.

Loach, B. and Bloor, C. (1995) 'Dropping the bully to find the racist.' *Multicultural Teaching 13,* 2, 18–20.

Lurie, D.J. and Zylke, J.W. (eds) (2001) 'Systemic vs individualistic approaches to bullying.' *Journal of American Medical Association 286,* 2, 787–788.

Mac an Ghaill, M. (1994) *The Making of Men.* Milton Keynes: Open University Press.

Mackridge, K. (2018) *Bullying, harassment and abuse at work – why the law needs to change.* TUC. Accessed on 11/02/2019 at www.tuc.org.uk/blogs/bullying-harassment-and-abuse-work-why-law-needs-change.

McAfee (2013) *Digital Deception: The Online Behavior of Teens.* Santa Clara, CA: McAfee – An Intel Company. Accessed on 25/04/2019 at https://www.anti-bullyingalliance.org.uk/sites/default/files/field/attachment/mcafee_digital-deception_the-online-behaviour-of-teens.pdf.

Milgram, S. (1963) 'Behavioural study of obedience.' *Journal of Abnormal and Social Psychology 67,* 4, 371–378.

Monks, C.P., Smith, P.K., Naylor, P., Barter, C., Ireland, J.L. and Coyne, I. (2009) 'Bullying in different contexts: Commonalities, differences and the role of theory.' *Aggressive and Violent Behaviour 14,* 2, 146–156.

Morita, Y. (1996) 'Bullying as a contemporary behaviour problem in the context of increasing societal privatisation in Japan.' *Prospects 26,* 2, 311–329.

Myers, C.A. (2006) 'Schoolbags at Dawn.' In F. Heidensohn (eds) *Gender and Justice: New Concepts and Approaches.* Devon: Willan.

Nassem, E.M. (2012) *Where Does Bullying Exist in Children's Everyday Experiences of School?* Doctoral thesis. Huddersfield: University of Huddersfield.

Nassem, E. (2015) 'Why do children bully?' *School Leadership Today 6*, 5, 68–73.

Nassem, E.M. (2017) 'The complexity of children's involvement in school bullying.' *Journal of Children's Services 12*, 4, 288–301.

Nassem, E. (2018) Bullying is still rife in schools. Here's how teachers can tackle it. *The Guardian Teacher Network: Lessons from Research.* Accessed on 21/08/18 at www. theguardian.com/teacher-network/2018/jan/17/bullying-is-still-rife-in-schools-heres-how-teachers-can-tackle-it.

Newberry, A. and Duncan, R.D. (2001) 'Roles of boredom and life goals in juvenile delinquency.' *Journal of Applied Psychology 31*, 3, 527–541.

Ofsted (2003) *Bullying: Effective Action in Secondary Schools.* London: Stationery Office.

Ofsted (2012) *No Place for Bullying.* London: Ofsted.

O'Kane, C. (2000) 'The Development of Participatory Techniques: Facilitating Children's Views about Decisions which Affect Them.' In P. Christensen and A. James (eds) *Research with Children: Perspectives and Practices.* Abingdon: Routledge.

Olweus, D. (1993) *Bullying at Schools: What We Know and What We Can Do.* Oxford: Blackwell.

Pikas, A. (1989) 'The Common Concern Method for the Treatment of Mobbing.' In E. Munthe and E. Roland (eds) *Bullying an International Perspective.* London: David Fulton.

Pritchard, R.E., Potter, G.C. and Sauccucci, M.S. (2009) 'Using sequential two-part focus groups as a supplemental instrument for student course evaluations.' *Journal of Teaching and Learning 6*, 1, 21–28.

Rivers, I. and Cowie, H.A. (2006) 'Bullying and homophobia in UK schools: A perspective on factors affecting resiliency and recovery.' *Journal of Gay and Lesbian Issues in Education 3*, 4, 11–43.

Rowe, W.S., Theriot, M.T., Sowers, K.M. and Dulmus, C.N. (2008) 'Perceptions of bullying and non-bullying children.' *Journal of Evidence-Based Social Work 1*, 2–3, 159–74.

Ryan, A. and Morgan, M. (2011) 'Bullying in secondary schools: Through a discursive lens.' *New Zealand Journal of Social Sciences Online 6*, 1–2, 1–14.

Schott, R.M. and Sondergaard, D.M. (2014) 'Introduction.' In R.M. Schott and D.M. Sondergaard (eds) *School Bullying: New Theories in Context.* Cambridge University Press: New York.

Smith, P.K. (2011) 'Why interventions to reduce bullying and violence on schools may (or may not) succeed: Comments on this special issue.' *International Journal of Behavioural Development 35*, 5, 419–423.

Sondergaard, D.M. (2012) 'Bullying and social exclusion anxiety in schools.' *British Journal of Sociology of Education 33*, 3, 355–372.

Spears, B. and Kofoed, J. (2013) 'Transgressing Research Binaries: Youth as Knowledge Brokers in Cyberbullying Research.' In P.K. Smith and G. Steffgen (eds) *Cyberbullying through the New Media: Findings from an International Network.* Hove: Psychology Press.

Stonewall (2014) *The Teachers' Report: Homophobic Bullying in Britain's Schools in 2014.* London: Stonewall.

Stonewall (2017) *School Report: The Experiences of Lesbian, Gay, Bi and Trans Pupils in Britain's Schools.* London: Stonewall.

Sullivan, K. (2001) *The Anti-Bullying Handbook.* Oxford: Oxford University Press.

Sullivan, K. Cleary, M. and Sullivan, G. (2004) *Bullying in Secondary Schools: What it Looks Like and How to Manage it.* Trowbridge: Cromwell.

Swearer, S. and Hymel, S. (2015) 'Understanding the psychology of bullying: Moving towards a social-ecological diathesis-stress model.' *American Psychologist 70*, 4, 344–353.

Terasahjo, T. and Salmivalli, C. (2003) 'She is not actually bullied: The discourse of harassment in student groups.' *Aggressive Behaviour 29*, 2, 134–54.

The Children's Society (2016) *Good Childhood Report.* London: The Children's Society.

The Independent (2017) 'Schoolboy, 12, found hanged after bullies threw meat at him for being vegan.' 29 September. Accessed on 21/08/18 at www.independent.co.uk/news/uk/home-news/louie-fenton-schoolboy-found-hanged-vegan-bullies-threw-meat-hertfordshire-inquest-a7973261.html.

Thompson, D., Arora, T. and Sharp, S. (2002) *Bullying: Effective Strategies for Long-term Improvement.* London: Routledge.

Walton, G. (2005) 'The notion of bullying through the lens of Foucault and critical theory.' *The Journal of Educational Thought 39*, 1, 55–73.

Walton, G. (2010) 'The problem trap: Implications of policy archaeology methodology for anti-bullying policies.' *Journal of Educational Policy 25*, 2, 135–150.

Willis, P. (1977) *Learning to Labour: How Working Class Kids get Working Class Jobs.* New York: Columbia University Press.

Wolke, D., Lee, K. and Guy, A. (2017) 'Cyberbullying: a storm in a teacup?' *European Child and Adolescent Psychiatry 26*, 8, 899–908.

Youth Justice Board (2004) *Key Elements of Effective Practice: Restorative Justice.* London: Youth Justice Board.

Zerubabel, E. (2006) *The Elephant in the Room: Silence and Denial in Everyday Life.* Oxford: Oxford University Press.

Index